"I encourage anyone interested in getting into the music industry to read this book."

Marty Hom, *Tour Manager, Fleetwood Mac, Barbra Streisand and Shakira*

"In the darkened shadows of the stage lies an entire ecosystem of professionals making magic happen. Not enough is written about the incredible opportunities of a career spent behind the curtains. In this book Matt gives the world a chance to see with finer detail the numerous paths that make up this dynamic profession and in doing so hopefully inspiring a new crop of young professionals destined to make the backstage magic happen."

Jim Digby, *Production Manager, Linkin Park; President and
Co-Founder, Events Safety Alliance*

Production Management in Live Music

Production Management in Live Music: Managing the Technical Side of Touring in Today's Music Industry is a handbook for the aspiring production manager looking to forge a career in the live music industry.

This book outlines the role that a production manager performs and their key responsibilities, and takes the reader step by step through the entire process of preparing a show for a tour. From dealing with artists and management to hiring crew, from booking vendors to scheduling the day-to-day of a busy tour, this text covers everything that is needed to take the show into rehearsals and finally on the road. Every aspect of the job is covered, including the very important challenges that face today's industry in the realms of sustainability, inclusion, diversity, and mental health. Whether the show be on a festival, in a small theatre or club, or in a modern arena, this book clearly lays out the tasks and challenges and offers practical solutions to ensure the smooth running of a live performance.

Production Management in Live Music is written for students in stage and production management courses and emerging professionals working in live music touring.

Matt Doherty has been working as a production manager for over three decades. From managing festivals to working on the international touring circuit, it is safe to say that production management has been his life.

Production Management in Live Music

Managing the Technical Side of Touring in
Today's Music Industry

Matt Doherty

NEW YORK AND LONDON

Cover photo: "Eclipse" by Simon Terrill 2008
First published 2022
By Routledge

605 Third Avenue, New York, NY 10158

and by Routledge
4 Park Square, Milton Park, Abingdon, Oxon, OX14 4RN

Routledge is an imprint of the Taylor & Francis Group, an informa business

Library of Congress Cataloging-in-Publication Data
Names: Doherty, Matt, author.
Title: Production management in live music: managing the technical side of touring in today's music industry/Matt Doherty.
Description: [1.] | New York: Routledge, 2022. | Includes bibliographical references and index.
Identifiers: LCCN 2021035191 (print) | LCCN 2021035192 (ebook) | ISBN 9781032138923 (hardback) | ISBN 9781032138886 (paperback) | ISBN 9781003231349 (ebook)
Subjects: LCSH: Concert tours–Production and direction. | Concerts–Production and direction.
Classification: LCC ML3790. D64 2022 (print) | LCC ML3790 (ebook) | DDC 780.78–dc23
LC record available at https://lccn.loc.gov/2021035191
LC ebook record available at https://lccn.loc.gov/2021035192

ISBN: 978-1-032-13892-3 (hbk)
ISBN: 978-1-032-13888-6 (pbk)
ISBN: 978-1-003-23134-9 (ebk)

DOI: 10.4324/9781003231349

Typeset in Times New Roman and Helvetica
by KnowledgeWorks Global Ltd.

This book is dedicated to my family who have always put up with me being away from home.

Contents

Foreword

When I was approached by Matt to write the foreword to his book I had very little idea on what to write and how to even go about it, as in my 45 years of touring and things this was completely new to me, so I sat down and had a good think on where to start and how to start. In doing this it took me back to my first days on the road where you had to learn new things every day so that is how I thought of writing this.

Life in the Music Business is the best job there can be but it is also the hardest. It is the most rewarding and the most demanding. Quite a bit like writing this foreword!

I guess what I am saying is this: I never had the help of a book like this on to show me the dos and the don'ts, so we all learnt as we went along, so I find that a book that deals with this, and the whats, the whys, and the wherefores of the Music Industry is very refreshing.

Most people think they know what goes on in this business through reading about Rock 'n' Roll acts in the newspapers, but that gives them very little knowledge of how it happens or why it happens.

So, a book that outlines this is a welcome idea. I suggest that you read this book from front to back and get an inside understanding of what we the crew do on a day-to-day basis.

Read it, digest it, and learn and this will stand you in good stead in your new career.

Jake Berry
Jake Berry Productions
Scottsdale Arizona
June 2021

Preface

I am writing this small book as a very simple guide to the basics of what can be quite a complex and exacting job. Complex and exacting, but also extremely rewarding. I intend to try and distil what I have learnt over the past three and a half decades into something hopefully easy to read, and understand, that will give you some clues as to how to act so that you may make your own journey and achieve some success as a production manager as I have been lucky enough to have done.

Acknowledgements

I would like to thank the following people who offered counsel and shared their knowledge with me as I took this journey.

Alexis Lowes, Dave 'Dash' Rowe, Debbie Taylor, Zoe Hodge, Evan Lawrence, Neil Zeagman, Jim Digby, Nicolai Sabottka, Mark Candelario, Mark Jacobson, Tobias Rylander, and Luke Howell.

And to all those veteran PMs, TMs, promoters, managers, agents, site coordinators, and production coordinators who taught me so much over the years.

Introduction

I have often said that you never know your professional journey has started until some years have passed, and this seems particularly true for our industry. So many established music industry professionals of today could tell you a story of how they dropped out of college, or they just hung around with their mates who were in a band, how it was a hobby. And now, looking back, they see that they have forged careers out of that; raising families and buying houses … you know … like a real job! My journey is certainly one of those stories.

Understanding this then, be aware that the path to this job is not a normal one, and to make things harder the conditions that existed for us old guys and girls are probably not always present today. This is a transitory time as our industry is learning how to educate and to train. So, you will find Academy X and University Y offering this course and that one. You might have friends who are in a band. You might not know what to do because the path is not immediately apparent. I hope it will be one day, but now alas, you need to work hard to find it. I am hoping to help you.

The established industry at the present time still very much cares about hands-on experience, rather than formal qualifications. This can and should change. However, it can only work when the educational side of the industry steps up and begins to provide graduates that are suitably job qualified. If you are looking to start out now, you need to understand this. We are always cautious about someone who has not *done* the work. But how can you gain experience without being given a chance with a gig? This is a ubiquitous issue across all industries, but in ours where the system of qualification is still in its infancy the problem is greater. I do not pretend to have the answers but I hope with time as the music industry continues this 'looking inward' things will change. Heck, I am writing this book as part of this process of change.

So this book is primarily aimed at the student and the younger person trying to find the path to a career in Production Management. I am going to discuss the fundamental skills that I believe are needed to do the job correctly. I will talk about the role as it is relevant to touring through clubs, theatres, arenas, and festivals as these are the places where you will be plying your trade. From the initial conversation with a client that leads to employment, through the whole show design process to the all-important advance, rehearsals, and finally to the actual show.

DOI: 10.4324/9781003231349-1

I state that, in this book, I will be talking about the methods I have used and am still using to manage the productions of my clients. You should be aware that this business, although connected in several ways, has for its history been a story of hundreds of, what are in effect, small businesses travelling the globe delivering their art to mostly grateful audiences. Hence there will be many different ways that this business is conducted. Nothing is set in stone. Deals for one artist may not work for another. One client will have their 'way' of doing business and the next client may do it differently. Be aware of this and be ready to adapt as I will often point out. Other veteran production managers may offer you different advice at times and that is as it should be. Be a sponge and from all this information learned you will develop your 'method' and if you do it right, it can lead to a successful and rewarding career. Maybe one day there will be a standard that everyone works by, but I for one hope the business retains the interesting and sometimes unusual methods by which it achieves its success.

The live music industry is a very young industry, if you realise, what we consider as a familiar 'rock show' has only been around for the past 70 years[1]. By extension, therefore, it is important to understand that many of the basic structures that are so much taken for granted in more established industries are in their very early stages in live music, or simply do not exist at all. Full regulation, a comprehensive training and education system to feed the industry, full employee, and contractor representation are some examples.

On the other hand, this business of ours is also quite advanced in many ways. We are so often tasked with achieving the very nearly impossible, and so are forced to find efficient and resourceful ways to do so. A bigger more extravagant show, a shorter timeline, more bang for the buck. We adapt what we have and we make what we need. We borrow ideas and technologies, develop them to our needs, invest in new concepts, all to the same end … the show.

As the demand for greater and more spectacular shows continues to grow, we push the limits and set new standards.

To say that the Live Music industry is full of talented individuals is quite the understatement. If you consider the path that most of us took to get where we are (and by extension the industry where it is today), it is truly remarkable.

I am not intending on this being the definitive treatise, because I do not see myself as the definitive expert, more someone who is lucky enough to have made and still is making the journey through this entertainment industry. I am very fortunate to belong to a small club of professional production managers. If you seek to join this club, then you should know that the standard is high and the road is a long one. You will start out in a vendor shop or as a junior member of a crew, in whatever discipline you have a passion for. Experience will come and you will grow. I can promise you that boredom won't be a part of your working life. It will be a challenging road at times but know that commitment is the most important ingredient for success, so commit to it and work hard and you can get there.

NOTE

1 The Moondog Coronation Ball was a concert that was scheduled to be held in March 1951 in Cleveland Ohio. Generally considered to be the first 'rock n roll concert', actually never got past the first song of the opening act due to the overselling of tickets.

C H A P T E R   2

My History

For me it was all about the music. I was not a good musician. In fact, I was dreadful. The band that I was in at school was a typical school rock band of the late 1970s, early 1980s. Two guitars, bass, drums, and keyboards. I played the saxophone badly and had bought a synthesiser. I could sing so I had the lead throat duties on two or three songs in the set. But it was obvious my skills lay elsewhere. I was the one who organised the rehearsal rooms, booked the gigs and rented (and set up) the PA (Public Address) systems. I knew that was why my friends let me stay 'in' the band. We progressed past our final year at school and were getting some reasonable gigs.

One day I headed early to the rehearsal studio to find a stranger in the room I had booked. He was setting up some keyboards. I enquired as to who he was and when he told me, I realised that my band mates wanted me to leave but did not want to tell me! I waited for them to arrive and then we had a chat. I was not angry at all. I knew this was beyond my talents. I suggested that I should maybe do the sound. They all agreed wholeheartedly!

I would have to say, that day was, in fact, my 'start'.

The next 12 months saw me attempting to gain entry to the business which meant, in reality, hanging around a particular pub in Melbourne on Saturday afternoons where the gentleman who I had rented PA systems from for my band had a regular afternoon gig. There was no money, but I would get some lunch, and I would in return help unload the truck and set up the gear. I learnt as I went and soon became competent at the set up and basic operation of the PA. Then, one Saturday my friend asked me if I could drive a truck …. 'No' was my answer. His response was to throw me some keys saying, "It is parked in the lane. After the load out this evening, drive it home and then be in Taralgon tomorrow at 10am". Now this was a challenge! Nevertheless, I managed to get moving and after parking the truck overnight outside my Mum and Dad's house, the next morning I crunched and ground my way some 100 miles to the venue and I was there on time. I got paid $40.00 for my efforts and I was officially working!

That became my job of sorts even though I was still studying. My week was made up of university and three or four gigs. The next step was when I got offered a proper job at an audio company. My first tour came soon after that. It was only 6 years of touring as an audio engineer before I did my first gig as a production manager (PM) in 1991, and then

DOI: 10.4324/9781003231349-2

began to concentrate on that role. I still occasionally stood behind a console but finally stopped mixing altogether in around 1994.

I am very fortunate to have worked with so many wonderfully talented people in my career. In my early years, I learned so much from the top PMs and their site coordinators (sitecos). There were festival promoters who supported what seemed like whacky and expensive ideas, stage, and production managers who understood that the job was about getting stuck in and working hard ... not just talking about it, brilliant crew chiefs who were communicative about what worked and what did not in my methods, the loyal vendors who always delivered and managers who knew how to let you do your job without micro managing you. This industry is about the people, always has been so, and I hope it will always be that way.

Production Management

What makes a good production manager (PM)?

If I had to pick one quality only, then it would be consistency. I am going to say this with the following caveat. It is expected that the core skills of production management are present in the candidate. That he or she can perform the tasks that make up the job .... Now for why consistency is so important.

Consistent performances sow the seeds of confidence. Confidence in you shown by your client, your crew, your vendors, the industry. How to achieve this consistency?

Now here is a tip from an old road dog. Address every issue as soon as it hits your desk or inbox. Do it straight away. This may seem like it will disrupt a measured and planned workflow ... and, yes, it will, but you should give up the idea of your own work day ever ending up as it was planned. You must jump and change and adapt constantly throughout your day in order to achieve *a planned and measured day for everyone else* .... **THIS IS THE JOB.**

The fundamental that underpins this is that the job of the Production office is one of SERVICE. You might be the boss, and I may have a whole chapter on leadership, but it starts and ends with this one key point. You provide the details, you arrange the resources, allocate the funds you are assigned by your client in the budget, map out the logistics, all of this to get to that one point in time ... the show. Once these things are sorted and in place and you begin the tour, your role then shifts.

Let's deal with the 'service' thing.

One fundamental for success for any crew member, technical or other; is this. Do the same thing at the same time each day. This leads to order and that is the foundation for a smooth production. In the same way a band rehearses to get their performance more polished, you and your crew will, in effect, rehearse your roles; firstly in the actual rehearsals, but also when the tour begins, with the early shows, ironing out any issues and making the flow of the build, the show, and the load out go more smoothly with each time it is done.

DOI: 10.4324/9781003231349-3

You have hired the crew, booked the gear and planned the trucking, travel, accommodation, buses, and freight, you have advanced the shows and now it is up and running you are just there to primarily make sure that all these components are working together efficiently. So in essence you are serving the show. I am told it is often the case that many PMs like to (and I will be kind here) 'lead from the front'. Usually with a constant barking of orders and directions. So, what is the point of hiring all of these experienced and skilled technicians, an excellent stage manager, top line riggers, etc, if you are going to direct all these functions yourself? If you have a dog there is no need for you to bark. You get my point. Micro-management will only result in resentment. Better that your crew know you have their backs and that if needed the big dog can start barking to back them up. It is my opinion that you are doing a better job by supporting the specialists that you have hired for your client. Helping them to do their job and being a constant in the background, ready to help more directly *if* needed.

THE EARLY DAYS OF THE JOB

Let us start with the client. Your first communication with the client will probably be a meeting or a conversation with the artist's manager or a representative of artist management, or in some cases your partner in middle management; the tour manager. This may be the person who will, more than any one person direct you in your job. You may have to present your budget to them. You will advise them on routing issues, or venues, on what can be achieved and, more importantly, what cannot be achieved. This person needs to be across EVERYTHING that can or will have an impact upon the artist. They need to be out front of any issue so you should establish at the outset which method of communicating they prefer. I live on email, but one of my clients loves to talk so I have to call him, and always answer his calls. Another client prefers texts prior to phone calls so with these two clients I only follow up with email …. Adapt, adapt, adapt.

You will strike a pay deal with your client. This will usually be a weekly rate for the tour and an advance rate for the pre-production you will do prior. I will advise you here to get to work immediately the run becomes available. Do not wait until the agreed advance pay starts. There are a few reasons for this which we will look at later, but start with the schedule or run of shows. Get to know the run intimately. Know the miles between the venues, know the venues. If you have not played them, do your research. Many advances will be conducted whilst already on the road, as the next leg gets booked, but for now let us assume that you are at home in your office and starting fresh with a new run of shows.

THE HOW

Let me say from the outset that this is my method and one that has served me well for years. There are other methods which obviously will work well too. I am happy for anyone to share this information that I have learned over the years. I firmly believe that at the present time, we are not doing enough to share our knowledge. This needs to change. Give out the information you gain and share the learnings.

How then do you start (and remember this is your decision ... no one is going to tell you to start)? See the chapter on The Advance for the details on this part of the job. The Advance is the time where you communicate with the promoters and exchange the relevant information (that you have prepared) so that the show can be installed at the venues and festivals that the agents book. It is my opinion that starting the advance too early can be counterproductive. No one is ready and the people you want to exchange information with are concentrating on shows that are happening sooner than yours. I start communications with the promoters one month out from the show as a general rule. *This timing needs to be different for festivals if your client is headlining as it is usual for the headliners to have some involvement in the design of the festival show. We can deal with this in more detail in the 'Festivals' chapter.*

TO RECAP

You have been hired and the deal is done. You are going to get started on the following areas now to avoid missing out. This may be many months out from the tour and as I mentioned the pay has not started, but off you go. Start with the five points below and then after that you have time to concentrate on the following:

- If a new show is proposed, then you have some involvement in the design process. (See the chapter on The Show)
- Editing and revising riders. These need to be brought up to date and revised for the appropriate markets.
- Compiling all the relevant and up to date specifications for the show into some coherent form ready to send to the vendors of record or out for bidding.

1.TRANSPORT AND FREIGHT

Trucks and tour buses are two of the most in-demand resources. These need to be sorted as soon as even the whiff of a tour comes out. If you don't hold them as early as this, you may well find you are missing out. And you cannot do a tour without trucks right? You can do a tour without buses but believe me, if you are in the USA or Europe, you don't want to do that. As I write this, it is the first week of December. Two months ago I got the news of some dates in Europe. I immediately contacted my preferred bus company in Germany to put buses on hold. This hold was for NEXT JUNE, NINE MONTHS AWAY. You guessed it, I am having trouble. It will be sorted out as the relationship with the vendor is strong, but you can see my point.

It is very important that you also get the routing to your trucking vendor not only so that they can hold trucks for you but very importantly, they can see the number of team or double drivers you will need. I am not going to outline the exact details of the hours that truck drivers can drive before a break, what sort of break it needs to be, whether it can be had in the sleeper cabin or has to be taken away from the truck. These laws are different in each major market and are changing all the time. My advice here is to stay as up to date as you can. You can usually download the regulations from the relevant government website or ask your trucking company. For the purposes of this section, it is essential that you have your trucking company look over the routing and highlight any issues so that you can take these to the client. There may be cost implications and you need to make your client aware now so that they can make adjustments if they wish or accept the costs.

If the tour is international then obviously the freight agent/forwarder needs to see the international moves, so that the necessary air or sea freight space can be booked if needed. For any move across borders the necessary paperwork needs to be organised and submitted (see the chapter on Trucking and Freight). So again, let your freight agent see the routing and highlight any issues.

2. TRAVEL AND HOTELS

Along with the trucking, freight and bussing vendors, send the routing to the travel agent immediately. Popular festivals (and indeed solo shows) attract visitors to the city where they are held and the hotels, especially those close to the venues, get sold out fast. So get your travel agent working on the hotels ASAP. Hold off on any crew flights as things change and often last minute. These can be done when the advance starts. It is less likely that the routing will change so you should get your hotels at least held immediately. It is often the case that a hotel will allow you to get out of a contract cost if there is a routing change anyway, but always check with the travel agent. You can use placeholder names or just hold a number of rooms sufficient for the likely final number of crew. You can always let rooms go. It is harder to get extras if you don't have enough held.

3. PRODUCTION VENDORS

It is a similar story for the various vendors. Gear gets booked, and therefore can be unavailable for the late caller. Hopefully, for you, the vendors are all long standing, and you have done some excellent work maintaining the relationships with them leading to very positive responses from them about the gear you require for the tour. If all is well then your various specs for this run are probably in need of an edit. Work with your departments to make sure the show is specified correctly. Check with management, and the show designer to see if there are to be any modifications and then send the up-to-date specs to the vendors for quoting. This is obviously with regard to an existing show design that is heading out again. For a new show on a new cycle, then a different game is afoot and you can learn about this process in the chapter on The Show.

4. CREW

I am sure many PMs can relate to this. I often feel I am an employment agent. It is rare in our business that people are employed under a contract or put on salary. Most production crew are hired guns who move where the work is. Band crew tend to be more static. If you are lucky enough to have a fairly static crew, then a whole period of the advance work is removed from your desk. If not, then you will have crew to find, vet, and employ. At the highest levels, it is quite common for a PM to have his or her team made up of production coordinator, stage manager, head rigger, carpenters, and other crew. Often time carpenters will move around from camp to camp with their stage manager. You would be getting the picture now. This is the ideal world; one where you can bring your team to a camp and all of you stay and work together as you have done for years. This works for the client as well for obvious reasons, but the ideal world is not often the one you will find yourself inhabiting as a young PM, so adapt and above all be out in front. Start early.

5. THE GEAR

At this early stage, if you are new to a camp, it is time to get an understanding of the equipment that is owned the client; the 'band gear'. A visit to the storage locations/s with one of the established band crew or the stage manager to go over it all. See if there are issues that need fixing and supplies that will need purchasing. Talk to band crew and get across the idiosyncrasies of this client's gear (there are ALWAYS idiosyncrasies). Identify if there are different rigs (A, B, Universal etc.) and see that the cases themselves are all in good order. This 'housekeeping' will serve you well on the tour.

It is very often the case that an artist will have a number of 'rigs', or fundamentally identical sets of equipment. Each rig's inventory made up of all the necessary equipment to do a show. The backline, the wardrobe, the set if there is one, and any ancillary pieces that are owned by the artist. The obvious reason for these duplicates is to be able to achieve time constrained routings, most often internationally. The B rig goes by sea to Australia whilst the A rig is working in the United States is an example. Careful management of this type of scheduling can saves many thousands of dollars. When we refer to a 'Universal' rig we mean the gear that cannot be duplicated and goes to every show. Think a special custom instrument or a guitar rig that has a certain sound that could not be copied into a B rig. The Universal rig is then obviously flying airfreight wherever the entourage goes.

For a young PM this can be a challenge to understand when and how to allocate the different rigs to the different legs of a tour. Seek advice from your freight agent. Talk with management about how things have been done in the past. Ask a veteran for advice. This is not the time to bluff your way through. The ramifications of a last minute 'move everything by airfreight' decision won't be good.

Leadership and Communication

LEADERSHIP

I often have found myself thinking that I need to be out on the floor of the arena or on the stage, or in the truck, or anywhere else other than in the office … and I guess I feel this way because that is where I came from. I learnt my 'gig' by actually being directly involved in the installation of the show; from unloading the trucks in the early morning, flying (or stacking) the public address (PA), and wiring up the stage, behind the monitor console through the sound check and the show, to the load out.

Some people are simply either not willing to be or even suited to the job of production manager (PM). I would like to assume that if you have gotten this far, you are, in fact, suited to it. I guess an indicator of sorts could be if you are not satisfied with your current position and are looking for more involvement in the bigger picture of the show.

NO MATTER THE SIZE OF THE PRODUCTION YOU ARE IN CHARGE OF, YOU ARE IN CHARGE OF IT

You cannot do an effective job of this if you get too involved in the nuts and bolts of the build. You need to lead this team of people. They are expecting you to do that. So, how do you go about this?

You are the crew's leader and should act accordingly. Firm but fair, and again CONSISTENT. If you act in the same fashion when you are presented with an issue time and time again, you will instil confidence in your team. Many years ago, at the end of a large arena tour, I remember asking one of the longstanding band crew how he thought the tour had gone and how he thought I had done as the new PM. His response was it was good to know that someone knew what was going on all the time. He felt safe. This makes sense if you consider that, to the untrained eye, the majority of a show day in any venue would seem like chaos. People charging about doing a myriad of different things. This crew member's comment meant a lot to me and I felt good that he had confidence in

DOI: 10.4324/9781003231349-4

me as a boss. Someone who could look at that 'chaos' and see a working team building a show, and achieving the timetable that was set. Once you have established this confidence, and this should be your primary task, you should then be thinking about morale. Let us stay with the confidence thing for a whilst though.

It is sometimes the case that the PM for a tour has gotten to that position by being a part of the crew for years and when the position becomes vacant is the next logical choice taking seniority into account, as well as aptitude for the task, and a good existing relationship with management and artist. How does this person take the new role and instil in his or her crew and client the confidence needed to get the job done without constantly being watched over or monitored? A difficult task it has to be said.

It will serve you well if you find yourself in this position to tread softly. Understand that you being the new PM may not be everyone's favourite idea. Understand also that you are being tested to see if the appointment was warranted. Stop and consider the state of things. Start with the show. Are there problems and if so where do they lie? Often times inexperienced managers will, in their attempt to solve a problem in a show, throw the baby out with the bathwater. Granted, it might be that certain crew might not be doing a great job, and it can be tempting to take this and accept it as the reason for the problem. But, taking some time to really look into the whole issue will serve you and your client in the long run. Has this crew member enough resources to do her or his job? Has the vendor either underequipped them or is the gear at fault? Is there actually a personality issue with another department? These questions need to be asked and answered. Although the problem may be in the automation department, for example, it is in fact *your* problem to solve. Taking a more measured approach will show that you are not a reactionary PM. Then when you make your decision, your crew and your client will know that you are not one to act rashly.

UNDERSTAND THE ENVIRONMENT YOU ARE WORKING IN

A lot of mistakes are made simply because the whole situation was not fully understood. Obvious words indeed.

The business of preparing, building, touring and managing a show is about people, and often times people under pressure. The artist feels the pressure to perform, and to satisfy many thousands of fans; every show. As is so often the case with creative people, they can find it difficult to relate to many of the things that we would see as normal and usual in our day to day. Add to this the expectations of fans, record companies, managers, band mates, etc., and you can see why sometimes artists are 'difficult' to deal with. I would not want that life for all the tea in China.

With this in mind, one can start to navigate the very often tricky world of working with people prior to touring and then on the road. A certain security director who is very successful and well regarded used to talk to me all the time about situational awareness. He was referring to how people are so often not aware of things even a few feet in front of them. We all know these types ... walking down the street head down staring at their phone ... no idea of what is actually going on. I am going to assume (safely, I hope) that you are NOT one of these people. Your job is to know what is going on, and because you are always watching, you become good at anticipating. You need to anticipate how people will likely react in many different and often tricky situations. Don't ask for a meeting about the creative whilst the band are in the studio tracking. Don't discuss crew wages before the tickets have gone on sale. Get good at looking at situations from the perspectives of others.

These skills and all the others I am banging on about are the contents of your 'toolbox'. Your judicious use of these in (here we go again) a consistent manner will make sure that you are prepared to deal with most any situation that is thrown at you. To remain calm in times of stress or if the client is upset, is only something you can do if you have this, head up, very aware, manner. Yours is not a role where knee jerk reactions will help you. You have an overview of the project that no one else really does and so it will behove you to keep this consistent calm approach at all times.

Years ago, as a young audio tech, I would hear time and again a tour manager or a PM tell us how they had done what we were doing and they understood how we felt. Usually these things were said during a particularly gruelling leg of a tour or during a difficult load in. They said this obviously to make us feel better about our jobs and the current conditions. You could believe that we were going into battle and our generals were boosting the morale of their troops. Quite like that really.

This is all good leadership. Don't be a PM who spends most of his or her time in the office frantically trying to get up to date with an advance. Here I will refer you to the passage in the 'CREW' chapter where I stress that you should get ahead as soon as you can so you can be free to monitor the tour and your staff to achieve the best possible result every day. It is out on the floor where you can get a gauge of how the crew are, what morale is like and if there are issues that need to be addressed. Talk to your crew chiefs. Ask questions. Be involved, and understand the environment you are in.

COMMUNICATION

My research has involved much reading and some very interesting talks with various industry veterans. One thing that came up a lot, was communication, and how the ability to communicate well was an essential skill for a PM. I completely agree. I believe that this one of many that a good PM must have or learn to have.

I like to think of a PM as having to be an Everyman because in the morning he or she will be talking to the truck drivers, and then the riggers, the local crew chief or steward, and the building manager. Later on the conversation could be with various crew, or the accountant and then the manager of the artist and then the artist. It requires a subtle shift each time to effectively communicate.

What we want to do here is simply to be able to communicate *effectively* whatever the situation. With regard to the tour, the truck drivers are not focused upon much else other than the loads and the routing, which is fairly obvious, but you are their 'boss' as well and so that means you need to lead them, and oftentimes inspire them to do their best work for the artist. It is a difficult and often thankless job, driving long distances each day and night in this business but you would be surprised at how spending some time with the drivers, getting to know them and letting them know how much you and the whole entourage appreciate their efforts boosts their morale.

I don't mean coming in all 'hot' talking about production this and famous person that. Rather you start the conversation and listen to what they have to say .... In my experience, truck drivers do like to talk, and you will make them strong allies if they know that you are a PM that listens. You will also learn a lot about this extremely important aspect of a tour. The 'skin' you wear when talking to the truck drivers will be different to the one you wear when talking to the artist. But you get my meaning. In a communicative sense, you must be accessible to all the people you work with and in a way that suits and appeals to them.

You can communicate with and be accepted by all the people you work with. Now we will deal with the next most important part of this. This relates to (yes) consistency. Each time any person on the tour approaches you, out on the floor, on the deck, in catering or in the office, they need to feel confident that they will get the same 'person' each time. This can be hard, but it is important to work at. Erratic behaviour or unpredictability is not in your remit as a PM. Remember that calm person who can deal with anything? That is you.

This is a part of that point about you shifting and adapting your day to ensure that everyone else (and by the extension the show) has a good day. If you start out with this in mind there will be little room for frustration. You can see how this underlines what I said in the previous chapter about starting early as well as what you will read in the chapters on the advance and the crew. All this points to be *able* to have the time to present this consistent front to the others on the tour, whether they are drivers, techs or the artist, you can only have this consistency in communication if you have prepared well enough.

CHAPTER 5

Key Relationships

Let us slow up a little and look at the touring entity that we call 'the crew'. Smaller tours may well just have a small team of a couple of backline crew who share the duties of 'teching' (a word peculiar to this business; from the non-verb 'tech'), the drums, guitars, DJ rig, and keyboards or however the band is made up, a sound engineer to mix the front of house (FOH) sound, a lighting director to do the lights, and a monitor engineer who mixes the sound for the band on stage. Often this core crew can remain with a band as they grow becoming what we then term the 'band crew'.

The as the band grow in popularity (if they are fortunate enough to do so), they will then need some middle management. The role of tour manager may well have been borne by one of the more experienced band crew in the early days and it may well be the same story for the role of production manager. This is fairly commonplace. But once an act starts to need a 'production' it will also need someone to manage that exclusively. By 'production' I refer to a lightshow, designed by a lighting designer and packaged for the road by a lighting supplier or 'vendor'. A touring sound system will be needed (which is actually two sound systems ... one for the audience called the FOH and one for the band on stage called the monitors). A video system if the act uses video content as part of their show, once again designed by a video designer and packaged for the road by a video supplier. Then there are the Special FX, the custom staging, the set, lasers, specialist rigging, pyrotechnics, automation, hydraulics, and any other systems that the designer of the show determines are needed to achieve the end result ... the show.

All these systems need trucks (or planes or ships) to get to the shows and then crew to install and service them. Then the crew needs stagehands and riggers to help them install all this equipment, and all these people, systems, trucks, and ancillary items need managing. The crew need transporting, either flying, or on a bus, they need accommodation, and feeding. These are the basics of the job of production management.

So, the crew now have grown from a small squad to quite the small army. And the schedule might be tight with many long days as we have mentioned.

DOI: 10.4324/9781003231349-5

And how does the production manager start to do this job?

The first and one of the most important tasks is to build the production team. Firstly the production coordinator. This role is one of the most important relationships that a production manager will have.

PRODUCTION COORDINATOR

The production coordinator has a tough job.

Quite simply the production coordinator runs the crew. He or she is there to shepherd the crew around the country, around the world. Hotels, flights, visas, buses, breakfast, lunch, and dinner, it is a huge job. The skill is in developing an encyclopaedic under-standing of cities, airports, hotels, travel times, bus driver hours, caterers, runners, just to mention a small number of the items that make up this job. Having a gun production coordinator can be the difference between having a happy and motivated crew or not ... back to the morale thing again ... so important.

> Let's talk about reputation for a bit. I am in the middle of a tour as I write this and as we were getting ready to go out, my regular coordinator was forced to jump off due to illness. As you can imagine this left me in quite a pickle.
>
> After a bit of a scramble, a good friend and colleague came up with a recommen-dation. This person was quite inexperienced but had done a few tours and by all reports would be up to the task. After a bit of an 'interview' over the phone, I hired her. Sure enough for the first few shows all seemed well. I was comfortable that things were going along nicely until one morning whilst on the last hour of a long bus ride, the tour manager contacted me to ask if I was OK with this person leaving the tour early. I was completely in the dark on this and then the tour manager told me she had found out about this on social media. As you might imagine, I was quite perturbed and confronted the coordina-tor who said, in quite a non-caring and calm fashion, that she had another gig to go to.
>
> I wont go into the rest of this encounter. Here you can see a young person, new to the industry, completely going about things in the wrong way. As I explained to her, this is a small industry and most of the people who do my job or who are tour man-agers (ie the hirers and firers) all know each other .... and we all talk to each other. So this young person suddenly realised that she was burning a fairly important bridge with her actions. Surprisingly she stuck to her decision to leave. My explanation that she was impacting her reputation was not enough to make her change her mind.

This cautionary tale is something you should take heed of. Your reputation is EVERYTHING. Until many years have passed, you are truly only as good as your last gig. So if you make a commitment to a project whether it be a tour or a festival, long term employment or short; KEEP YOUR WORD.

Some management of smaller artists do not like to pay any advance wage to a coordi-nator, so you may find that the entire advance is down to you. I, and I know a few other production managers who think similarly, like to book the crew hotels and travel for my crew party. I find it helps to really cement the run into my old brain. Once done I hand it over to the coordinator to manage.

If you are fortunate to have budget for pre-production for a coordinator, then do that early stuff together. The hotels, the travel, the visas, etc., but then let the coordinator take over the management of all of it leaving you to deal with the next part of the process which is the technical; working with the vendors and key crew to decide how the show is made up and how it goes together.

THE STAGE MANAGER

This is probably your most important one to one relationship next down from the client. The stage manager (SM) is the person who has a primary function supervising the actual build and dismantling of the show every day. He or she will work with the template you create for the show build, for labour and trucking, etc.

This is also my favourite job. On tour it is often the time I am wishing I was out on the floor building the show. The SM is the organisation's connection with the big cost centres of any production, the labour, the trucking, the venue, and the vendors. A poor SM can make a good production falter; a good one can both save money and make it zing! I have had the very good fortune to work with some brilliant SMs and I must say when you and the SM 'click' it makes your job so much more satisfying. A lot of the relationships you have on the road will work with excellent communication. For the SM (and for the production coordinator, and the tour rigger) it needs more than just good communication. When things are right, there is a trust there built from an understanding and a respect for the person and the role. Work hard to make this relationship strong and you will reap the benefits.

The SM will manage all the labour and all the crew as they come together to build the 'jigsaw puzzle' that is the show. Each SM has their 'way'. Their system of allocating the resources need for the build. We will deal with the labour in another chapter, so for now let's look at what is often called 'real estate'.

As the term implies, this is all about the allocation of space. In any venue, from the smallest club to the biggest stadium, a touring production requires a large amount of storage space as well as a large area to house the equipment that is essential to run the show. Lighting dimmer racks, video control, audio amp racks, SFX gear, steps, front fills, offstage floor lighting, automation landing areas, the monitor desk, and all its ancillary equipment all usually positioned around as well as on the stage. B stages, barriers, mix, and control positions all fill up the available space rapidly and it takes a good eye, an experienced SM to know how to allocate this in a logical fashion. To this issue of space, add the god of time and concentrate both and you have the SM's day.

> Often now it is the case that a large production will tour with its own stage or stages with all the show centric departments built into the stage structures, as well as the various 'gags' that are part of the stage. This is a great way of saving space and also has the advantage of looking more streamlined to the audience. However, this is also an expensive way to tour as it obviously involves more trucks and crew, not to mention the cost of the construction, or rental of the stage itself.

You should have a thorough understanding of your show's 'back end', not just the out front stuff. Let the SM do their job here and again be that support role. The talent here is to have a three-dimensional view and understanding of the stage and backstage and know where everything needs to be to ensure it can play its part. The efficiency is in the order of installation and removal. You can and should be looking to learn if you are fortunate enough to work alongside an experienced SM. From the empty cases for the floor lights to the actual set, every single component of the show has a home mapped out.

Not just in charge of the installation and removal of the show, the SM still has the more traditional connection to the performance and so is responsible for the different elements that are not static. Moving sets, satellite stages, other performers on and off, lifts, and gags, as well as working to support wardrobe for quick changes, etc. For the bigger shows they are often supported by an assistant SM/s and the team of carpenters will carry out the actual physical work, supervising the show call of stage hands.

It is indeed a long and busy day for a SM. Work closely to assist them in their role. Make this one of your critical partnerships.

THE PROMOTER REP

When you get the routing from the agent and you have the list of promoters, you send out a message to them all asking for the promoter rep contact. This is the first part of the advance and is covered in that chapter. Now who is this person? The promoter represent-ative is the person who is the first point of contact for you from the advance to the load out. You will send all the information to them and they will make sure everything that is needed locally will be gathered together for the engagement. Local labour numbers, the backstage furniture, the plant and other equipment, the catering if local. Every tiny piece of the 'local' puzzle. You can imagine how this role would scale up for the big shows and scale down for the club or theatre date, but the job remains the same.

> *It might be that the promoter rep who is assigned to work with your show is a PM like you but who has come off the road. Looking after the local venues is a good semi retirement role for an older PM. (Although I can hear so many reps laughing at my suggestion that is a job for semi retirement, with the industry being so busy I usually hear the story of how much busier these fine people are now that they have come off the road) My point here is that this is a gift. You can learn so much from the indus-try's elders and if you are lucky enough to get to work with some of the incredible veteran girls and guys who now call promoter representation their job, then dont miss the opportunity to learn. If you have your advance together and the show require-ments are dealt with, then there will be time to talk and I encourage you to do so!*

The promoter rep will (or should) meet you at the first call, update you on the sales, and cover off any local issues that need to be addressed. They will have similar meetings with the other middle management. It may be that the tour accountant needs a cash injection, and the venue security director will want to go over the procedures for the artists arrival and departure. There will be the VIP event people wanting to find their space, catering staff questions, runners' floats and vehicles, and we have not even started the walk! You get my point. The promoter rep has a busy day. Get them a radio and let them do their job to help your team build the show.

CHAPTER 6

Touring Staff

All tours of any reasonable size are broken down into parties. A, B, and C.

A FOR ARTIST, B FOR BAND, AND C FOR CREW

We spend our workday with the C party, but there are several important roles in the A and B parties that you need to know about, as you do work closely with them. You are the senior person in the C party, obviously, so knowing 'who's who in the zoo' is essential for the good communication that is so important to a tour's success. If the artist IS the band then there is only an A party and a C party. If the artist is a single principal with a hired band then you have all three parties, you get the picture.

The people on the tour.

TOUR MANAGER

The tour manager (TM) is your partner on the tour. He or she is looking after everything relating to the artist whilst you are looking after everything related to the show and the crew. Having good communication with the TM is critical and you should work hard to establish a good relationship from the outset. It may be that, with the artist you are working for, the TM is senior to you, or you are equal or, in fact, you might be senior. Whichever way it is, get a good system of communication in place during the advance; be it weekly meetings or at the very least, regular phone calls. As you are proceeding through your advance the TM is proceeding through theirs. Whilst you are sorting out what vendor bids to accept and what crew are needed, they are looking after the artist's needs for travel, accommodation, and day to day requirements. I am sure at some point an excellent TM will write a scholarly tome on this role and relegate the production manager (PM) to a chapter or section, but the fundamental I am trying to get across to you is this. You work together as the middle management of the organisation and are the people on the road who will decide the day to day for the entire entourage. Yes there may be tours where you (or the TM) are lucky enough to be joined by an accountant or by a road manager to help spread the responsibilities, but often it is just the two of you, so good communication is absolutely essential.

DOI: 10.4324/9781003231349-6

TOUR ACCOUNTANT

This person has a fairly obvious role managing the accounting of a tour, doing the settlements with the promoters, collecting invoices, and authorising payments to vendors. Your link to the accountant is through the production budget and you will need to be transparent with all your deals and negotiations. Stay out in front of this relationship. Make sure you are up to date with your 'paperwork'. Often when there is no tour accountant, the TM takes this role on. And if you are starting work (in your advance) before anyone who has that role you will be dealing with management and business management to prepare and manage the production budget. When the hand over happens then make sure that you have everything ready and available for the accountant. Being methodical and precise in this department will go a long way for you in your career. Once again, be a good communicator.

ROAD MANAGER

Sometimes a bigger tour will have a road manager. This term is used nowadays for an assistant to the TM, whereas in the past it was the same role. If it is a big tour with multiple parties then sometime a road manager/assistant will come out to help the TM with that.

SECURITY

One person or a whole team. Security usually break into two key departments. Artist security (or 'personal' or 'close personal') and venue security. For the biggest tours there is often an advance security team, but not something you will need to worry about for a few years! It is usual for the venue team to travel with the crew party and the artist team obviously would travel with the artist party. You need to work closely with venue security, as there is much in their day that affects yours and vice versa. I go into this in depth in the chapter on security, but for now, know that the range of involvement for you goes from doing pretty much everything if you are not touring with any security, to just making sure there are bus berths, hotel rooms, as well as office space, and all necessary support from your office on the road.

ANCILLARY A AND B PARTY STAFF

Depending on the type and size of a tour, you may find the hallway populated with various 'staff' who may work directly for the artist, for one of the artists, for management, or for the promoter, the designer, or just be a friend of the artist who has a role on the road.

WARDROBE

There may be a single wardrobe person on the tour. There may be a team of five or even more. These talented individuals have a high-pressure job and need support. Get the head of wardrobe involved in the room allocation early and learn what their specific needs are. If I can impart one tip for a PM to best support the wardrobe department, it would be; give them as much time as you can and as much space as is available for their needs. It is not brain surgery to work out that a good day for the artist does indeed include a good wardrobe experience.

CATERING

Whether to tour catering or not may be a decision for you, or it may be from the artist. It might just be the way it always has been done in the camp you are working in. My own preference is not to carry catering. I believe that using local caterers helps the local economy as well as reducing the number of people and gear touring. But that is for another chapter. If you are carrying catering, then obviously you are carrying caterers. The kitchen needs to be built EARLY, so be ready to support this installation with crew and energy. The caterer will have done their own advance with the venues but you should be offering every assistance here to ensure a smooth install ... it is breakfast we are talking about and getting your crew fed is one of your top priorities always.

It may be that you don't have touring catering but do have a catering coordinator (my preferred option). This individual will do an extensive catering advance also to ensure that the tour's catering needs are met, and also usually manage procure all the dressing room food and drink, general backstage hospitality, and bus stock. Make sure this person has a desk and work space in or near your office, the necessary cases, a runner in each town, and the necessary funds to do their job. It may well be that there is a private chef on the tour to cook for the artist. Here the same level of support. Find out what is needed and make sure these things are covered either in their own direct advance or through the catering advance. An excellent way to find out if someone is behind on their advance is to offer them help.

MASSEUSE/THERAPISTS/TRAINERS

Not much to say about these roles. Fairly obvious really. Not usually too involved with your crew party. But need to have them on your room allocation list.

VIP/MEET AND GREET TEAM

Depending on the nature of this 'event' then you may have a couple of people on the road dealing with the VIP event or the Meet and Greet. Many artists look to these sort of events as an important income stream. Here your involvement will be about time and space .... Get it done early, and make sure the VIP crews are well aware of all the issues so that the artist will have a smooth event.

DRIVERS

Yes, the drivers of the trucks, the buses, or indeed the splitter van are all in fact part of the crew. Although not directly involved in the show itself (unless you have drivers doing follow spot), we would not be calling house lights and ushering the artist to the stage without the hard work of these individuals. A young PM can learn a lot from a good driver. So many of these fine ladies and gentlemen have decades of experience and love to share their knowledge. Start with simple things, like making sure the truck driver meals are delivered on time during the load out and are top notch, and that when you get up in the morning on the bus you make the driver a coffee.

TECHNICAL CREW

The following departments operate separately, overseen by the stage manager. I have spoken of the interconnections that exist between them, and how they all work to the same end, but the actual internal operation of each department is controlled by the crew chief or department head. Depending on the size of the show there will be more or less of the roles that I mention below.

AUDIO

This department is usually headed up by the FOH sound engineer. This position has a system engineer as a direct assistant. Then there is the monitor engineer, and the stage tech/s, the fly crew (SL and SR) then on the bigger shows there are the delay crew/s as well as an RF tech. Like the other departments that have vendor crew in them, the size of the team is dictated by the size and complexity of the system. Think scale up and scale down.

LIGHTING

Headed by the lighting director, this team is as big as the light show requires it. A larger arena show can have six or eight LX techs, led by the crew chief. Different positions are dimmer tech, truss/rigging techs, floor lighting techs, you get the picture.

VIDEO

Headed by the video director, this crew may just be building one screen, or ten screens and a full live camera package with a large directors' suite. Made up of a crew chief, enough LED techs to cope with the size of the LED screen, projector techs (if there are PJs), camera director, engineer, Robo Cam CCU, server tech, server op, enough camera techs/ops for the number of cameras.

RIGGING

If you are touring a large show then you will have a tour rigger. Depending on the number of points then there may be a second or a third or a fourth working with the lead. Most touring riggers are fluent in CAD and will usually do their own advance with buildings to ensure that the rig can either fit as it is designed or be adjusted slightly to fit. One of the most important relationships you will have on the road is with your rigger.

CARPENTERS/SET

A team of carpenters will be needed to build the set and various other items of the show that do not fall under the remit of any other department. It is often the case that the stage manager will have his or her team and so will bring them to the tour depending on requirements. You may have a hydraulic specialist in this team if the set is complex like that so the term 'carpenter' is used loosely. Good carpenters also assist the stage manager with the load in and out ... generally making life easier for everyone.

PYRO/SFX

If the show has pyro and/or special effects then you will have a pyro team, and/or an SFX team … handling the SFX equipment, gases, powders, and various other ingredients for the SFX component of the show. There will be extra needs for this team so get on the front foot and make sure they have what they need. Permits for the dangerous or explosive materials are obtained by the vendor and they will do their own advance with sites and venues, but you should be copied in on all this correspondence.

LASERS

If the show has lasers as part of the creative package, then you will obviously have a crew to install and operate them. It is on the outdoor show where this department will need extra support from you to ensure that the necessary permits are secured. Have the laser vendor send through the various safety documents and risk assessments as well as the approvals so that you have copies.

AUTOMATION

If the show has anything automated in the rig, then you will have an automation crew. They usually work in closely with the lighting and rigging departments, but if it is SFX that moves then they will work with that team … you get the picture.

BACKLINE

The band's crew. The backline department are there in whatever numbers the makeup of the band requires. Usually one tech for each musician … although sometimes one tech can look after more than one musician. If there is playback as part of the performance then a Pro tools tech (or whatever platform the artist uses) will be a part of this team. It is often the case that a musician member of a band will have had the same tech working with her or him for many years. Be aware of these long-term relationships. If you are coming into a well-established camp as the new boss, having good relationships with long standing backline crew is a great way to learn about the camp.

MERCHANDISE

The company contracted by the management to distribute and sell the merchandise for the tour will on a tour of any reasonable size send a 'Merch person' out, as one of the crew party. On the smaller of these tours, you will need to allocate some truck space for the merch rolling stock, where on the bigger tour merch will have their own truck/s. You will probably have to find the merch team bunks on crew buses and hold hotel rooms for them; although it is usual that they will pay their own bills here, so stay in touch and keep the communication channels open.

OTHER CREW

As shows become more innovative and complex you may find yourself carrying a more diverse crew than I have gone into as artists seek to set a new benchmark in entertainment ... drones, inflatables, VR, AR ... all in play. Learn what the needs are. Learn that your role is to support the show ... however it is made up. Remember the section on 'service'?

Stadiums

The outdoor stadium show is the largest scale of a solo show that we do, and to take that on the road is the biggest challenge of the lot. To wit, you will have a whole raft of different crew members on the team. I won't go into the minutiae of this as it would be logical to suggest that if you are touring a stadium show you don't need this book! But for the sake of knowledge, here are some of the outdoor specialist roles.

Site coordinator (Siteco)

Here is the boss of the outdoor, in charge of the installation of the stage and other structures that are required for the show's production to be installed in a stadium. In the stadia environment, this means dealing with access, finding space to actually build the stage. In years gone by we used to lay roadways made from plywood so that the trucks, forklifts, and importantly the cranes could drive over the sacred turf of the stadium. Fortunately today there are systems of portable roadways for heavy vehicle access and also pedestrian friendly grass protection systems for the main field where the patrons will be. The Siteco will run the steel build schedule, booking the various calls of labour from basic stagehand calls to the more specialist calls of climbing steel hands, scaffolders, and riggers. He or she will also be the main point of contact with the venue, to allocate (or indeed sometimes, build) the dressing rooms, deal with the seating vendor (if needed), install the local production (think maybe extra audio delays sourced locally, or audience lighting if there is an outside broadcast involved). Everything that will make the stadium ready for the Production to install the show.

Steel

The term refers to pretty much everything that makes up the stage structure that travels with the stage system rather than with production. Very large stadium tours will often have multiple sets of 'steel'.

The steel crew usually come from the staging vendor and will have a crew chief, and a number of steel crew, most of whom will be riggers as well as scaffolders. Working under the Siteco, they often will be one team of two or even three where they will 'bunny hop' around the country or the world installing their stage for every second or third show.

Overnight

Often times you can compress a build schedule on a stadium show. This means you have double steel crew, and the build continues around the clock. To supervise this then the Siteco will usually have an overnight person come and run the night shift. And the promoter will have an overnight site team in this case to mirror the touring schedule.

Advance

Often for a stadium show it is wise to do an advance visit if at all possible and get the basics understood between the promoter's representative and the tour. Basics like access, location of boneyard, dressing rooms, and general backstage, delays positions, grass cover, etc. If this is the case then often the PM would be accompanied by the security director and other concerned department heads to make sure of things for their departments. If the tour is ongoing and a busy one there may be an advance person that runs ahead of the tour; a bit like a human version of my advance summary notes!

I have covered here all the main staff positions that tour. Just like with so much else, there is not a standard for this, and you may well find yourself on the road with some people who I have not covered here but who your client has decided are important enough for a berth on a bus.

CHAPTER 7

The Crew

"There is nothing more important than morale."

Many people, who have not worked in our industry, seem to think that our job is 'cool' and glamorous. Those that do know understand that this is far from the truth. The schedule of a show day CAN run from 5 AM to 2 AM … that's 21 hours. Even with breaks and the fact that most crew will not work that amount of time with some breaks away on the bus, etc., it is still a physically demanding, and mentally challenging job. Experienced crew tend to wear the difficult times like a badge of honour. They will tell you about the time they did five, six, seven, or even ten shows in a row. They exude a pride in the fact that they did it, the show went on. This is a recurring theme … weirdly.

How did they get through these long gruelling stretches of shows?

I like to describe the structure of a touring crew outfit as a benign dictatorship. Managing a large group of people, who for all intents and purposes 'live' at work is a challenging job. You may have inherited a crew. You may have put the crew together yourself, or it may a combination of the two. For me it is all about personality. It may be that guitar tech so and so is the best in the business but if he or she has a bad attitude then it will be like a cancer in the crew and will soon cause trouble. It is your responsibility to see this and fix it. Here your real 'management' skillset comes into play. Let's examine this for a bit.

It is said that the first rule of good management is; do not give someone a job that they cannot do. Apart from the obvious message in this, it basically means that everything is your fault! And it is. I have made the mistake of giving someone a job that was beyond them. You may well also. Look at the context of this. Just recently on a co headliner tour I was chatting with the other camp's production manager. The topic of discussion was the huge challenge it was to find someone good for a vacant crew position. It is very often the case that crew move on or are let go for varying reasons and they need to be replaced. When this happens actually on a tour, it is a real challenge as there can be very little time especially if the crew member has been fired; either by the artist or by yourself. You cast the net, and you rely on resumes and/or recommendations from others. There is not much choice in this during the busy season as everyone is usually busy, and if they are not then you have to wonder why.

DOI: 10.4324/9781003231349-7

You should do your best to keep a crew working well together. You should accept that people are different and that means that you have to work alongside people who may have different values and ethics than yourself. Be tolerant. See the positives. Don't become the doorman on a tour that becomes a revolving door of crew changes. And look hard at a situation where someone is not fitting in or performing at the required level. Rash decisions to send people home can cause headaches in other areas.

In reality most every problem can be solved. Interruption of a negative flow will force reflection and allows new ideas to be inserted into the stream. Just like the switching of a breaker will open or close a power circuit, you must be prepared to be the 'circuit breaker' when a production faces problems. And I am not an advocate of the above-mentioned revolving door. Interrupt the situation. Examine the current methods and look for changes and solutions *with the people and resources at hand* as a first instance.

This method is not infallible. And yes, it may be that after all this hard work to find a solution to the problem, the problem still remains. Then, as any good manager must, you will have to make a decision to remove the problematic crew member. But this should always be a last resort in my opinion.

So be involved … watch the relationships in your crew develop or not … and monitor the mood. To be in a crew that is fighting is to be in a toxic work environment, and it is your responsibility to ensure a healthy work environment. In a 'normal' job, a person gets to leave at the end of the day and, in many cases, go home to people who love them. In the touring game, that is not possible as the crew who may have been arguing during their work hours might have to live on the same bus. They don't get to leave for weeks or even months. I have just sat down to write this having left a fractious situation that was developing in my lighting crew. The crew boss was giving one of his guys some grief about being a team player. The crew member was confused as he had been told by the Lighting Director that he needed him to concentrate on a different area and make that his own. A lot of people would be fine with this confusion … grumble a bit and work it out. However, people are different and this particular chap was/is someone who needs structure. The methods that the crew chief was using were not working so it was time to step in and bring some order. Key here was not to be seen to be on anyone's 'side'. You are the mediator, and no good comes from yelling at people. Encouragement and cajoling to get people back in step. Their morale is key to them doing the job properly. A little time for them to settle back down, check on things again and then you can get back to your other work.

Here you can see how much management is needed once a tour is on the road. This example highlights how critical it is to get your advance in order in a timely fashion. How can you possibly monitor and be aware of important issues like these if you are stuck behind your desk constantly trying to catch up?

PRESSURE AS A TOOL

I talk about how crew rehearse and get better at the load in, the show, the load out. Now I want to talk about pressure. There is a saying in this business that the time spent working on the task will expand and compress in line with the time allocated to perform it. Put more simply, if you have a whole day to load in and set up with no show, then your crew will take the whole day to do that. If you give them five hours on a show day, they will take five hours. To do the same job. Strange right?

We joke about this. We get frustrated by it. Managers and accountants will question you because of it. But, IT still remains. In my view the answer/difference is obvious; Pressure.

How often have you heard someone say that they perform well under pressure? I will leave it to someone a lot smarter than me to do the study on this and return with the statistics. For now, you should know that oftentimes pressure is your ally. I am not talking about times of drama or incident that were not planned and bring new constraints of time to your day. No one wants these unwelcome incursions.

I am talking about using pressure to help you train. Now this may seem all very obvious, and maybe it is, BUT there are times when you can make a scheduling decision that will bring some welcome pressure to bear on your situation. Knowing when to do this (and by 'this' I mean adjusting the schedule or changing the plan) is of course something that will come with experience but as with anything that we learn, we have to understand the why before we can be good at the when.

Back in the days of The Big Day Out I used this method a lot. The promoters had scheduled the first five shows with enough time. We had a Production day and so our set ups were methodical and organised with little stress. The sixth how however was not so easy. Held in the city of Perth on a Sunday after the Adelaide show was on the preceding Friday ... yes, I know; 2800 km between the two cities and one day and 24 trucks to do the crossing.

I do not need to go into the Perth load in ... needless to say it was fast! My point here is that we used the load outs of the other shows as training for this one all-important Adelaide load out. The main touring production was 33 trucks and when we hit our rhythm we could have that lot out in 3.5 hours. So we loaded out the Goldcoast show as if it were Adelaide, the Sydney show the same and so on. I used this pressure to get the crew good at the process of going that quickly SAFELY. Practice is the only thing that can make that happen.

Examine your show, examine the routing. See where the pressure will be brought to bear because of time and then bring it to bear earlier in the routing to TRAIN.

If, however, it is coming at the crew every day as the show is too big or over designed, then you need to look at how you can help the crew establish a workable routine that will safely install the show without problem. Seek guidance from a mentor or consult with the stage manager and department heads. If there is something that needs to change to achieve a schedule or a show build safely, it is down to you to identify this and take it to the client for permission to make the adjustments. It is not acceptable to think that it will all just get better. Obviously here I am talking about something more than the refinement of the load in and load out times due to practice. It is your responsibility to maintain a high standard of safety and if something in the show is causing this to be downgraded, you must address it.

If it seems that I am harping on about time (or lack of it) an awful lot, it is because good production management is all about time and the allocation of it. I have a whole chapter on time and how it rules your working life ... but for now back to the crew.

They are called the 'crew'. An individual is a 'member' of the crew. It is like a club. There is a pride about being in the club. Special merchandise is produced for the crew, with the words 'crew' embroidered on to set out apart from everyone else's merchandise. Understanding all this, you can harness the spirit that comes from that and use it to make your crew more efficient and simply better at their jobs. Obviously this leads to a better production, a better result for your client, and a better result for you as you chart a course through this business.

The Stage

Let us look at the different types of stage; the platform upon which the artist performs. The following are ones that you will most likely be building the show on, over, and around.

CLUBS

There are so many club stages in the thousands of clubs around the world. Some bigger, well run and longstanding establishments have decent stages with proper backstage facility, and alas a lot more do not and you make do. Typically the club stage will be an 'end stage' which as the name suggests has a back wall and the sides are usually used for gear with the audience to the front. This is where most of us learned the ropes. Never enough room, never enough height, invariably a challenge. I would suggest however, that a lot of crew's problem solving skills were honed in the clubs of their early careers.

THEATRES AND HALLS

In this type of venue, the stage that you will most often encounter is correctly called a Proscenium Stage, and as you probably well know, is divided up into areas:

- The Apron
- The Stage proper
- The Wings

The stage proper and the apron are demarcated by the Proscenium which is the arch over the downstage edge. This traditionally has an ornate fascia and frames the stage from the front, for the audience's gratification.

The area downstage of the arch is the apron. Upstage of the arch is the stage proper. Why 'down' and 'up' stage? Traditionally a stage was raked. That is, it slopes downwards from back to front. So you go 'down' as you head to the front of the stage and 'up' as you go to the back. Stages were designed like this to assist with sightlines … ensuring that the audience in the upper balconies would be better able to see the whole performance.

DOI: 10.4324/9781003231349-8

You still see this rake in most every theatre of any age that you go into. Modern buildings usually build the stage flat, but the terms of upstage and downstage are still how we refer to location onstage ... on any stage ... club, theatre, arena, stadium, or festival.

Traditionally theatres will have an orchestra pit downstage of the apron, where, as the name suggests, the orchestra lives during a performance. Sometimes the pit can be raised up to be level with the apron. Then this area is called the forestage.

Stage left is obviously the opposite side to stage right! TV people call it Camera Right and Camera Left. It is the reverse because the camera 'looks' at the stage from the house and the show 'looks' at the stage from the stage. In the theatre the two sides are called 'prompt' and 'opposite prompt' ('OP'). This was because the person who would 'prompt' the actors for their forgotten lines lived on that same side of stage every show (stage left) and the other side was lazily called opposite or off prompt or just OP. See Figure 8.1.

That deals with the 'deck' level. Now, let's look up.

The traditional system of rigging in a theatre involved the lowering in and hauling out of wooden battens that ran the width of the stage. Painted backdrops would be fixed to these battens and so the backdrop would change with the change of scene. Set pieces would be wheeled on and off to match the scene. The system of battens and the ropes, pulleys, and counterweights combined were referred to as the fly system. They were operated by flymen.

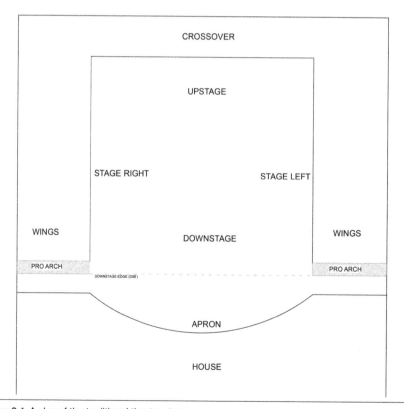

Figure 8.1 A plan of the traditional theatre stage

With very primitive methods as described, the clever part of this system was in the height of the space above the stage, or the scene loft. The many different painted back-drops would hang up there once 'flown out' obscured from the audience view by the proscenium arch.

As time passed, these systems were upgraded from wooden battens and simple ropes to metal pipes and wire ropes and then onto more sophisticated winch systems. The basic working principle remained the same however. When you work in an old theatre take the time to go and have a tour of the fly system if it is still intact (often is and used regularly). Often you will find you will be using the fly rig for your light show and drapes, or a com-bination of chain hoists and trusses that you are carrying and some of the theatre system.

THRUST STAGE

As the name suggests a thrust stage protrudes out past the pro arch (if there is one) and has audience to three sides. A tricky stage to put a rock n roll show on. Occasionally you will find that in a newer arts centre style establishment that stages all types of perfor-mance you will find yourself with a thrust stage. It is hard to just leave that space unused. As long as the lighting can get over and in front (and this is almost always possible) you are fine. It is not bad, just different.

AMPHITHEATRES

The oldest 'configuration' of the performance space is the amphitheatre. What we refer to as an amphitheatre is based on what the ancient Greeks used. (The word 'amphitheatre' comes from the ancient Greek).

A semicircular arrangement with the 'stage' central to tiered seating on one side, as shown in Figure 8.2, with a more modern version during a load in shown in Figure 8.3.

Figure 8.2 Greek Amphitheatre on Ios island

Photograph: Vasilis Ververidis.

Figure 8.3 Berlin Waldbühne amphitheatre

Photograph: Nicolai Sabottka.

Although the Romans also used amphitheatres for entertainment, more often these were a full circle of tiered seating rather more like our modern stadium (see Figure 8.4).

Today the amphitheatre is a very popular venue for live music (especially in the United States where they are often referred to as 'sheds') and some of the iconic venues we all know and love are in fact amphitheatres; the Hollywood Bowl in Los Angeles, Red

Figure 8.4 Roman Amphitheatre in Verona

Photograph: David Zean.

Rocks in Denver, The Sidney Myer Music Bowl in Melbourne, the Milton Keynes Bowl in Buckinghamshire are a few examples.

In some amphitheatres the stage is a temporary structure. If it is indeed a fixed stage then it is more theatre-like for this type of venue, being usually at one level. Often the amphitheatre will resemble a large theatre in most technical aspects other than it is basically an outdoor venue. A fixed stage at one level, wings and often a redundant scenic loft where now there is just the grid to take the flown rig of the touring production.

Now we can examine the more modular stages that can be built to the size required by you and your client.

ARENA STAGES

There are a few different indoor stage systems that are used widely around the globe but the principle is the same. Modules of 8′ × 4′ or similar size which lock together to provide a stage deck at the very usual 60′ wide × 40′ deep with heights between 5′ and 6′. There are many different sizes used today but this 60′ × 40′ (18 m × 12 m) size is one of the most often used. Most every arena (apart from a very few older and seldom used ones) own and operate their own stage and will have it in the configuration required for the load in time … (or very close to it!!).

> As we have discussed, a busy A level Arena will be going from sports to music to events to music etc. The stage will in all likelihood have just been placed as you are walking to the floor to start the rigging mark up. That is if you are using the house stage. Oftentimes the stage will be built out on the floor and wheeled back under the rig, but lets just assume you are using the house stage and it is in place when you start. A good rigger will first check the position … and if it is square to the room. This is vital and should be obvious to anyone involved, but you would be surprised at the number of times I have found the stage to be in the wrong position. Remember the section on understanding the environment that you are working in? Well the house crew may have been working through the night, and this may not be the first such night for this week … people are tired and working under pressure. If it is wrong then shortly you have a team of fresh stagehands coming on and they can help the house move the stage if that is what is needed. There is no advantage here to being a shouty type who just stands and insists on having what was agreed … just help fix the issue.

TOURING STAGES FOR ARENAS

Very often the stage is part of the touring production. Although obviously more expensive because of the extra crew, trucking, etc., it is often essential to the design of the show. Various components of the show will live inside the stage and the whole system can be constructed out on the floor down from the flown rig. Once the flown rig is up the stage can be pushed into place, saving an enormous amount of time, and allowing shows that probably would be pushed to make sound check time after a normal load in to do exactly that.

THE OUTDOORS

Either for a festival or for a stadium show, the outdoor stage and roof has come a long way. From the humble bandstand to the rickety scaffolding structures we saw in the 1970s through various incarnations to the modern roof and stage systems of today. The principle areas are the same. The stage, the wings, etc. One difference here is that it is mostly on the one level, so more like a theatre stage than an arena stage. That said the dock for an outdoor stage needs to be at truck height so that level will obviously be lower than the stage level accessed by a system of ramps. Issues that present for the construction of an outdoor stage and roof are many but let's look at two.

We have all seen rock documentary footage from years ago where the rain is pelting down and people are scrambling to throw simple tarpaulins over gear exposed on a stage where the roof is more a gesture than an actual roof. Over time the outdoor stage roof developed mainly because of two things; weather and weight capacity.

I will need to simplify this next bit for the lack of time and space. Suffice to say that the stage was the easy part as it was usually constructed from scaffolding and the way to 'deck it out' went from a primitive system of wooden bearers and boards with a plywood top, through the slightly more sophisticated scaffold plank sitting on transoms with a plywood deck to a custom system as in the 'black deck' system which did away with the hundreds of scaffold planks or boards and used steel members (Ones, Twos, and Threes) to make up the basic module. The development of this over time has lessened weight and made the system more flexible but it is still based on the same fundamental concept.

Then to add a roof. The early concert roofs were a series of trusses spanning between scaffolding towers. The main constraint on this system was the distance that a piece of truss could span. So bigger trusses were constructed to span greater distances. Bolted or strapped together to form a grid, the truss 'roof' was covered with a tarpaulin and pipes and clamps were used to tidy the whole thing up. It was hung by installing cat heads on scaffold towers and using chain hoists that were inverted to pull the roof up in between the towers. The front towers had beams installed at the correct height and the sound system was flown from these. The whole system was simple and reasonably strong. It was, however, not very weather proof.

To make the stage 'all weather' meant adding more sheets of tarpaulin or 'skins' as they are often referred to. The development of systems of extruded profile (usually in aluminium) to fix large skins together made it possible to build back and side walls for the stage. These systems were refined as was the actual roof, to make it stronger and easier to install and also weather proof. Like everything in our business it was important to not only make things strong and weather proof but also quick to build. The use of hydraulic rams to pump up towers, cranes to lift truss towers, roofs with inflatable crowns to assist the water runoff, all these refinements made the outdoor stage bigger, taller, and stronger.

You cannot, however, safely just build a wall and tie it into a roof without consulting an engineer. The more surface area (of skin) that you give a structure the higher the risk of failure due to wind load. You are in essence adding 'sails' that will act exactly as those on a ship and pull the structure in the direction the wind is blowing.

The various design adjustments that were developed to deal with this included, using water tanks or other weights as ballast to hold the structure down, re-designing the roof from the flat face rectangular structure to more of a domed structure and then tying that roof into the actual stage deck structure as ballast, using guy wires from the roof to concrete weights to stop twist or lateral movement, to mention just three. The engineering of a roof and stage structure is a complex and critical task. The role of the engineer is one of the most important in the outdoor event business. Standards are rightly high now and all outdoor structures in the main markets are certified as well as being 'signed off on' by an engineer when installed for a show or festival. The engineer will visit and inspect the structure to make sure it has been constructed according to the plans that she or he signed off on originally to allow the construction. Yes there are still places where you will find stage structures that are quite obviously not up to spec, and these are to be avoided. As I state in the Health and Safety chapter, there is a disparity in standards and some countries do not take stage structural safety as seriously as they should. It is good to learn some of the fundamentals in stage building, at least so you can recognise when something is not right. A wander below the stage deck will reveal a lot about a structure.

Mobile or 'truck' stages got over a lot of the permitting hurdles of other more substantial stages simply due to the fact that they were on wheels, thereby being assessed under different criteria to build stages. These stages were quick to install and cheap but had limitations due to their size and capacity. Like everything else, however, mobile stages have been refined and developed to allow greater loads and through a clever navigation of the rules they have bigger add on deck areas making them able to compete for the bigger shows with the more traditional stage and roof systems.

When you play on a festival or outdoor show, have a look at what type of structure the stage and roof are and talk to the steel crew about it. A good time to learn at least some basics. I am lucky for the period when I owned and operated a staging company in Australasia to have had a brilliant engineer who taught me a lot about structural safety and what to look for. I encourage you to seek out some further knowledge in this field.

CHAPTER 9

The Advance

Now you will build your advance. Here comes the consistency thing again. Every tour you do, you should use the same approach. My favourite method is to use a cloud-based file sharing service like Drop Box. Then you only have to update one thing and everyone will see it. There are a few similar cloud-based file sharing services and I am sure some of them are great. I am familiar with Drop Box and so use it consistently and exclusively.

Just before we start with the nuts and bolts of the advance, let's see what 'tools' are needed for you to do your job.

THE SCHEDULE (ROUTING)

You will be sent (or you will need to ask for it from the agent's office) a run of shows with the promoter contacts on it. Usually, these contacts will be the actual promoter and so you will need to send out an introductory email to all of these contacts asking for the details of whoever is to be your promoter rep, or day of show contact.

In my opinion it is important that you be the first one to contact the promoters. Establish a chain of communication and it will leave less room for mistakes. You can introduce your colleagues in the opening exchange. I list all the important contacts on my advance sheet and they are also in the relevant riders.

The first contact will be made usually in the lead up to the on-sale. See the chapter on this topic for more … for this section we are talking about the technical advance.

I like to get this started one month out from the show. This allows the other departments time to get their advance underway. It is definitely not a good look to make your colleagues rush their advances because you are disorganised. If your show is not a new one and you have toured it for a while, then there is no reason not to get your initial advance done quickly so you can concentrate on other things. If it is a new show and you are still in rehearsals or yet to start them, it is wise to let the promoters know that things can and probably will change.

DOI: 10.4324/9781003231349-9

THE RIDERS

This is the term that refers to the appendix or addendum to the contract between the artist and the promoter. There are usually legal, technical, hotel, security, and hospitality riders.

You should get the most up to date riders from management and then you will need to edit the ones you are in charge of thoroughly to make sure they are relevant to the markets and venues you are going to be playing. Having been on both sides of this, I can tell you it is frustrating to be sent an irrelevant rider by a production manager (PM). It just adds unnecessary work. If you are playing theatres, it is useless to send an arena rider, as it is just as useless to send a theatre rider to a festival promoter. Therefore, you will need to adapt what riders you are given to suit the tour you are going on. Then a conversation with management about what the artist expects and what has been promised by the promoters. By this I mean … Are you headlining? Are you doing the whole show? How long is the show? Who is providing what? And most importantly, who is paying for what?

Once these issues are clear, you then need to make sure that the document is not only relevant to the show but also covers all your requirements.

You would have heard the saying that there is no such thing as a dumb question. I firmly believe that this is so especially in the context of this job. You may feel that you are constantly asking silly questions but ASK THEM! Get the directions very clear from the outset and if possible get them in writing. The agent has done the deal with the buyer and often this is where they leave it. Work with the agent to gain a clear understanding of the deal for the tour or the show. Know very clearly what the agreed terms are with the promoter. Go into your advance armed with this knowledge.

Let us explore this with regard to a busy festival. You are the PM for just one of many acts that are playing, and therefore you are going to be put into a prioritised list by the festival management team. To assume that one thing or another will be looked after is to walk on thin ice. Check and double check that you will have everything you need to put on your artist's performance. It will be you explaining why not to the artist if you leave this to chance.

In today's world of a million emails and rammed inboxes, most festivals are now adopting an online advance portal where you log on and upload all your riders and requests. I am really not a fan of this system, not because I am old (well sort of) BUT because your artist is playing the festival bound by the terms of the contract between the festival and the artist. Usually, any performance is contracted around the nature of the show and therefore according to the technical and other needs of the artist. Once you and the festival step away from this arrangement, by going online and using the aforementioned portal, you could now be in a grey area contractually. It may make things easier for the festival staff BUT it simply means more work for you as you MUST check that each of the things the contract has in it for the performance are mirrored in the online advance process. If they are not it is up to you to make the festival and your management aware so this can be fixed. No one else is going to do it. The agent won't know unless you tell them and then they can go to work for the artist they represent. Get your agreements that are outside the online advance in writing before you move forward.

Work with the tour manager (and catering coordinator if you are lucky enough to have one on the crew) for any changes to the hospitality rider. Have security send you their most up to date security rider. Get these documents together with the technical rider, the advance sheet, rigging plot, stage plan, and any other specifications that are appropriate (e.g. if it is a festival, your audio specification will be needed also) and send them off to each promoter rep on the list. Here is a little tip. Understanding that whilst you are doing the right thing and waiting until your tour is on each promoter rep's radar, you also are very much aware of how busy this business is all year round, so I always ask in the message of the initial email that a response is sent immediately to acknowledge the receipt of all the information. It is not enough to think that simply because you have hit send, the job is done ... follow up in whatever way suits you, but make sure you follow up; to ask if everything is understood and there are no red flags.

THE ADVANCE SHEET

This sheet is a time saver. Full disclosure I borrowed this from a friend (thanks Spider), as I liked its simple layout and how it contains all the needed info in one place. Basically it is a form that gives the promoter much of the necessary information on one page and has space for them to fill in all the vital venue-related information for you. See Table 9.1 for an example.

Although it seems like a lot, it is actually a very simple way of asking all the key questions and at the same time pointing out the key aspects of the show. I always use one of these sheets and have different versions for small club size gigs, theatres, halls, arenas, and stadiums. You are not asking for a steel boneyard for a theatre show, etc.

Once the promoter rep has filled it out, I upload it to the relevant show folder in the drop box so all staff can see it.

When I get to the advance phone call, it makes things go quickly when I can just run down the sheet.

Table 9.1 Sample of an advance sheet

ARTIST NAME				TIMES
VENUE INFO				
CITY:			OUTER DOORS:	
			INNER DOORS:	
DATE:			OPENER 1:	
			OPENER R 2:	
VENUE:			SHOW:	
ADDRESS:			CURFEW:	

PLEASE INCLUDE A MAP AND DETAILED DIRECTIONS OF HOW TO ACCESS THE VENUE WHEN YOU RETURN THIS SHEET

TOUR PRODUCTION

NAME	ROLE	CELL	EMAIL
	Production Manager		
	Tour Manager		
	Production Coordinator		
	Tour Accountant		
	Venue Security		
	Catering Coordinator		

VENUE

NAME	ROLE	CELL	EMAIL
	Production Service Mgr		
	Fire Marshall		
	Production		
	Catering Manger		
	Security		
	Box Office		
	Merchandise		

PROMOTER

NAME	ROLE	CELL	EMAIL
	Promoter		
	Tour Coordinator		
	Production Director		
	Promoter Rep		

VENDORS

NAME	ROLE	CELL	EMAIL
	LIGHTING		
	AUDIO		
	LASERS		
	AUTOMATION		
	TRUCKING		
	VIDEO		

(Continued)

Table 9.1 Sample of an advance sheet (Continued)

SCHEDULE	
DATE	
Traffic Control	-
Venue Access / Call Back	-
Catering load in	N/A
RIGGING CALL	6:00AM
LIGHTING LOAD IN	7:00AM
Venue Fork Lifts	THREE
Lunch	12:00PM
Set Barricade	
SOUNDCHECK	4:00pm
Dead Stage	-
Dinner	5:00PM
Doors Outer	
Doors Inner	
OPENER 1	
OPENER 2	N/A
ARTIST ON STAGE	
Load Out	N/A
Curfew	N/A
HARD	
FINE	

Loading area Access:
Please keep the loading area totally clear of alien cars, and clean

Chair Set/Cleaning:
IF the gig is not General Admission..he entire arena floor should be clear of chairs, with set up to be schedule at 2.00pm.
After the show the arena floor should be cleared of chairs as quickly as possible

Washer & Dryer:
Production is carrying and will need hookup early.

Garbage cans:
Place 240lt Garbage cans around the stage and backstage area

Signs

Medical staff:
There must be at least one Medical team in the building for the show

Doctor On Call:
Please have an ear nose & throat doctor on call

Date:	RIGGING	LX	AUDIO	VIDEO	SET	BACKLINE	Show Call	Load Out
Time:	6:00AM	7:00AM	9:00AM	10:00AM	10:00AM	12:00PM	7:00PM	10:30 pm
Runners			3					
Head Rigger	1							1
Rigger Up	18							18
Rigger Down	6							6
Crew Chief	1							1
Stage Hands	8	18	12	12	8	4	4	54
Pushers		8						8
Truck Loaders	4	4						12
Fork Lifts & Drivers	1	2						3
FOH Spot Ops		0						0
Wardrobe Assistants			1					1
Catering Runner			1					
Electrician / House Lights		1					1	1
TOTAL	39	33	17	12	8	4	5	105

(Continued)

Table 9.1 Sample of an advance sheet (Continued)

SECURITY ADVANCE				
	PLEASE HAVE VENUE SECURITY GET IN TOUCH WITH SECURITY DIRECTOR			
	AFTER READING THE SECURITY RIDER			
VENUE TYPE?				
DRAPE	Rear House Drape is required to cover entire width of the venue behind stage. Unsold seats are to be			
VENUE STAGE SKIRTING	FRONT OF THE STAGE MUST BE COVERED WITH A SUITABLE OPAQUE BLACK DRAPE.			
STAGE SIZE / AREA	*60ft wide x 40ft deep x 5ft high*			
STAGE PLACEMENT	*PLEASE SEE THE STAGE DRAWING IN THE DROPBOX INDICATING THE REMOVAL OF*			
	• CORNERS PRIOR TO LOAD IN			
STAGE LEFT WING SIZE	*NONE*			
STAGE RIGHT WING SIZE	*NONE*			
B' STAGE, THRUST, & EGO	*NONE*			
WINGS				
BARRICADE	YOU SUPPLY BARRICADE			
	Please have venue person present for positioning gate with aisles.			
RIGGING				
HEIGHT TO LOW STEEL?				
POINTS DS OF PROSCENIUM?				
RIGGING POINTS & WEIGHTS	SEE RIGGING PLOT IN THE DROPBOX			
RIGGING TOTAL WEIGHT	TBA			
ROOF BAY SIZE?				
OFFICES:	1 Production			
	2 Tour Management			
	3 Management			
	4 Security			
	5 Accountant			
	6 Wardrobe			
DRESSING ROOMS	Please have venue staff available to move furniture as required.			
	1			
	2			
	3			
SUPPORT				
CREW ROOM				

(Continued)

Table 9.1 Sample of an advance sheet (Continued)

NOTES:			
DB LIMIT?		#FORK LIFT	
NUMBER OF TRUCKS **15**		SPOT LIGHTS **NONE**	
NUMBER OF BUSES			
NUMBER OF DOCKS?:		LAUNDRY?	
PUSH DISTANCE TO STAGE?:		SHOWERS?	
POWER			**VENUE POWER**
LIGHTING: 1	400AMP 3 PH X 2	USL AND USR	
VIDEO: 2	250AMP 3PH	USC	
AUDIO:3	200AMP 3PH X 2	SR & SL	
		USL	
SFX NONE			
EFFECTS NONE			
FIRE EXTINGUISHERS NONE			
GAS REQUIREMENTS 4 x CO2 - VENUE TO PROVIDE			
2 X 20LB CO2 TANKS (NON SIPHONED) PER SHOWDAY FOR HAZERS			
PYRO PLAN NONE			
PRODUCT & PLACMENT NONE			
CONTACT NONE			
MISC FURNITURE / TOWELS / GROUND			
WHITE BATH TOWELS	120		
WHITE HAND TOWELS	12		
BLACK HAND TOWELS	24		
SOAP			
CATERING Catering Coordinator will be in touch to advance all catering and backstage rider requirements			
ARTIST GROUND ADVANCE Production Coordinator will be in touch to advance any runner/GT requirements			
FOR PRODUCTION: PLEASE HAVE 2 COPIES OF A SOLD SEATING MAP SHOWING ALL HOLDS, KILLS, GUEST SEAT HOLDS, FOR PM ON ARRIVAL			

ADVANCE SUMMARY NOTES

As I just mentioned, with a new show, you probably won't have started the rehearsals before the advance, so there is room here for some additional notes to explain the changes (if any) and to summarise the key points. A simple one- or two-page document. This will make it easier for you and more importantly for your team and avoids a million further emails. Here is a sample of that document.

ADVANCE SUMMARY NOTES

IMPORTANT CONTACTS

Here I list all the main points of contact from the tour:

VEHICLES We are in 15 trucks and 10 buses

STAGE 60′ × 40′ at 5′ high

POWER

Lighting	2 × 400 AMPS	USR AND USL
Video	1 × 400 AMPS	USC
Audio	2 × 200 AMPS	SL AND SR

FORKS 3 FORKS

FOH MIX POSITION

A reminder that we require the VIP/GUEST area in front of the mix position.

STAGE

A reminder that we require removal of the DS corners of the stage PRIOR to load in.

RUNNERS

4 RUNNERS: 1 @8:00 am (15 pass), 2 @9:00 am (2 × minivan), 1 @11:00 am (15 pass).

GASES

1 × Bottles of Medical Oxygen with masks and regulators.

4 × 20 LB **NON SIPHONED** CO_2

DRESSING ROOMS

We will pick rooms on the walk in the morning.

SUPPORT

The Support act is travelling in one bus with a trailer.

THE FX AUDIO SYSTEM

As you will see on the rigging plot in the drop box we have a second audio system. This is an FX system. It is essential that all seats are off the floor so we can rig this. It is also very important that there are enough house crew to remove the chairs immediately post show to pull this rig down.

LABOUR

See Table 9.2. Often not everything in the design works first time and things need to be ironed out … That is what technical rehearsals are for after all.

Table 9.2 The labour calls to go with the advance summary notes

Time:	Rigging	LX	FX audio	Main audio	Set	Video	Backline	Show Call	Load Out
	5:00 AM	7:00 AM	7:00 AM	9:00 AM	10:00 AM	10:00 AM	12:00 PM	5:30 PM	10:30 PM
Runners									
Head rigger	1								1
Rigger up	24								24
Rigger down	8								8
Crew chief	1								1
Stage hands	8	18	8	12	8	12	4	4	64
Pushers		8							8
Truck loaders	4	4							12
Fork lifts and drivers	1	2							3
FOH spot ops		0							0
Wardrobe assistants				1					1
Catering runner				1					
Electrician/House lights		1						1	1
Total	47	33	8	14	8	12	4	5	123

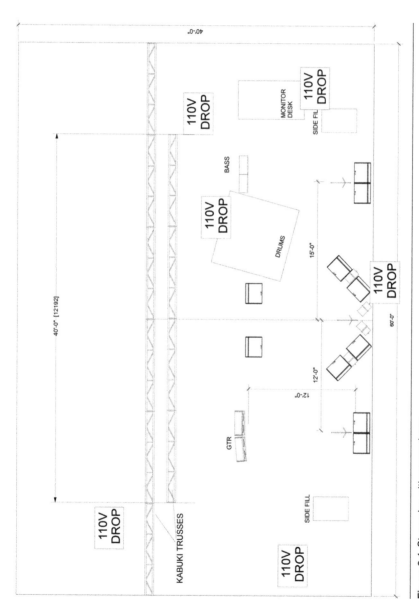

Figure 9.1 Stage plan with power drops

THE TECHNICAL SPECIFICATIONS OF YOUR SHOW

Let us assume at this stage that the show is designed already (we will deal with show design and how that affects you in another chapter). You will have a set design, lighting plot, an audio spec, a stage plan, maybe a video plot/design, and plots/plans of any other component that is a part of the show.

Now it is up to you to open the communication with the various promoter reps. A standard email attaching the riders, the technical information, and the advance sheet for solo shows or the riders and the various tech specs if you are doing a festival run. Have a look at Figure 9.1 and you can see the sort of information you need to send out on a stage plan. This is for a festival and I have noted the various power drops which the promoter will provide, as well as the critical dimensions. Obviously, if you are touring production and doing solo shows you do not need to send the stage plan, or the detail of the other specs, as you are carrying all that, but for a festival or a show with promoter supplied equipment then everything needs to be advanced, from the stage plan to the audio input list.

At this point I find it useful to put together what I call an Advance tracking sheet. A simple spreadsheet with the run of shows and the promoter rep contacts plus a list of checkboxes for 'tracking' indicating if you have sent out information, if you have received venue information, if the advance sheet has been returned and if you have had the advance phone call with the promoter rep.

Running in sync with this list, you should set up a folder containing files for all the shows and here you put all the relevant venue and show information that you get or are sent. And, you guessed it, all this lives in the drop box. Once you have a start on filing of all this information, it is time to invite all your crew and other management to share the tour drop box folders. Then they can all see the advance as you build it.

I have been harping on about consistency a fair bit. Here, in your advance, is where your colleagues will develop a trust in your methods as each advance you do is built in the same way. This takes time and some effort, but as I said earlier, you need to start as soon as you have the run and are confirmed for the job, not waiting for the first pay day.

I do not think I need to show you a sample advance tracking sheet. It is time to put those Excel skills to the test.

Sample Rider

Here is a rider from quite a recent tour (2019). As it states it is for an USA Arena tour. This is what I mean about writing riders that are specific for your tour. This same tour moved onto Europe and then to Australia and South America. For each region the document was edited to match the power services used, the truck sizes, even the system of measurement ... imperial or metric. I spent a good deal of time on the other side of this situation, working for a festival where we were sent many riders. Too often we would get sent a rider that was pretty much irrelevant for our situation, and this just added to the advance time. Do the right thing here and make sure you send relevant riders to each different promoter and region.

US ARENA TECHNICAL RIDER

There are so many riders out there and you would have read a few hundred of them I guess. How do I make this one stand out? I would like to think that you will be reading this in a relaxed state with a cup of coffee in hand and your feet up, alone without any disturbance, but I am dreaming I know. Please, do read the entire document, as it is pretty important to us that you do. Soon you should receive an invitation to our drop box as well wherein you will find the details of the show. If there is anything in either this document or the drop box that you don't understand, please call or email to ask your questions. We can solve most any problem given enough time.

Don't fret ... we are nice people and we are completely across the fact that we are in the entertainment business ... no ending of poverty or cures for cancer come from this line of work!

I am looking forward to working with you.

Many thanks

Matt Doherty

DOI: 10.4324/9781003231349-10

What you (the PURCHASER) have agreed to provide for us (the ARTIST)?

PROMOTER REP

The PURCHASER agrees to provide a representative with decision making powers in all matters, including occurring expenses and disbursements, to be at the venue one hour prior to the load in time, and to be available at all times for the ARTIST production department until the load out is complete and the ARTIST's crew has left the venue.

STAGE

The PURCHASER agrees to provide a sturdy and well-constructed stage built according to accepted standards, inspected and signed off on by an accredited structural engineer. The stage must be clear and free of debris or storage. There needs to be a minimum of 60' of clearance from the stage deck to the low steel.

Stage size 60' × 40' @ 5' high

The PURCHASER agrees to provide two sets of stairs to access the stage; placed stage left and stage right. These steps must have handrails, be secured to the stage and have step lights. They should NOT be attached to the stage prior to load in but should be nearby, to be placed by the ARTIST'S stage manager.

BARRICADE

The ARTIST may be touring a stage barrier. We can deal with this in the advance. If the ARTIST is not touring a barrier, then the PURCHASER agrees to provide a mojo style certified crowd barrier across the stage front, the wings, and around the mix position.

CHAIR REMOVAL

The venue floor must be kept clear of all obstacles for the load in and again for the load out. All chairs must be removed prior to the load in. They must be removed as a matter of priority IMMEDIATELY after the show finishes to help with the load out. All labour allocated for chair placement and removal must be independent of stage crew calls.

MIX POSITION

The PURCHASER agrees that the front of house mix position shall be placed 110' from the DSE (measured to the front of the mix). It shall be 24' wide by 24' deep. Audio will occupy the front 12' and behind this the PURCHASER will supply a riser 24' wide by 12' deep at 1' high for lighting, video, and laser control.

SIGNAGE

The PURCHASER agrees that no signs or advertisements shall appear in front of, on, or over the stage.

The PURCHASER agrees that, regardless of venue sponsorship, all its lit signage and all LED strips, rings, and screens will be turned off for the duration of the performance.

HOUSE LIGHTS

The PURCHASER agrees that the ARTIST'S production manager shall decide the 'walk in' light level.

The PURCHASER agrees that the house lights will go to full black out when called by the ARTIST'S stage manager. Please inform the ARTIST'S production manager of any safety or aisle lighting that must remain on for reasons of safety. We will require this to be kept to a minimum. Also, all vomitories and access tunnels to the arena floor and bowl need to be draped, to reduce light bleed into the house.

PARKING AND TRANSPORTATION

Total Vehicles

    16 × 53′ trailers

    10 × buses

    3 × 15 seat passenger vans

Please arrange a secure and well-lit compound where we may stage our production vehicles prior to be called to load/unload. This area must be available to the ARTIST one day prior to the show (should the ARTIST be arriving on a day off).

ALL tractors and ALL buses will require shore power.

If the parking area is not adjacent to the backstage area, then the PURCHASER agrees to supply:

Transport between the parking compound and the venue.

Toilet and washing facilities.

32 bath towels for the truck drivers.

Shore power all buses and tractors.

The PURCHASER agrees to make arrangements for the ARTIST'S trucks to have access to their load in positions one hour prior to the first call time, and that any permits or escorts which may be required are in place.

The ARTIST production may wish to make use of ALL AVAILABLE entrances to the venue. The PURCHASER agrees to send a detailed drawing of the venue showing all entries and relevant door opening sizes.

LOAD IN

It may be that the ARTIST'S production requires a pre-rig on the day before the show. The ARTIST'S production manager will advise about this in the advance.

The PURCHASER agrees to make the venue available to the ARTIST production at least 14 hours prior the doors opening time (notwithstanding the above note on a possible pre rig).

The PURCHASER agrees to advise the ARTIST'S production manager of any unusual aspects of the load in (stairs, elevators, narrow entrances, uneven or rough surfaces, etc.) in writing 14 days prior to the engagement.

The PURCHASER agrees that during periods of inclement weather, arrangements will be made to have the load in area clear and free of any snow, ice, or rainwater.

The ARTIST'S production will require all available storage. Please ensure that the backstage is not full of equipment not related to our engagement.

PLANT AND EQUIPMENT

The PURCHASER agrees that all plant and equipment requested by the ARTIST'S production shall be for the exclusive use of the ARTIST'S production for the duration of the load in and load out.

The PURCHASER agrees to supply two forklift trucks with a lift capacity of minimum 6000 lbs and a reach of minimum 12'.

LOCAL PRODUCTION PERSONNEL

All call times and numbers will be confirmed by the ARTIST'S production manager in the advance.

The PURCHASER agrees that all stagehands, riggers, and others will be under the direction of the ARTIST'S production staff. These personnel shall not be utilised for any other purposes unless authorised by the ARTIST'S production manager.

All working personnel involved with the show must be drug and alcohol free. Anyone found to be under the influence of drugs or alcohol MUST be removed immediately.

The PURCHASER agrees that all local production personnel will have, or will be provided with, the correct personal protective equipment (PPE), in line with relevant health and safety legislation.

The PURCHASER agrees that all local production personnel will have been inducted and have had all necessary toolbox talks prior to the call time.

Appurtenant staff

a. Electrician

The PURCHASER agrees that the venue/site electrician will be on hand at all times throughout the installation and removal of the ARTIST'S production.

b. Cleaners

The PURCHASER agrees that a full team of cleaners will be standing by to lean/clear the arena floor immediately after the show.

c. Medical

The ARTIST will require medical cover throughout the entire period of the engagement. The responsible lead paramedic or similar must make themselves known to the ARTIST'S production coordinator upon arrival.

Local Crew Calls

Appurtenant Staff

Load In

8 Loaders

72 Stagehands

24 Riggers

2 Forklift drivers

3 Production runners

1 Catering runner

1 Wardrobe assistant

Schedule

These times may change in the advance but this an indicative schedule.

CALL	TIME	CREW
MARKOUT	05.00	HEAD RIGGER
		18 UP RIGGERS
		6 DOWN RIGGERS
		4 LOADERS
		8 HANDS
		1 FORK
LIGHTING	07.00	16 HANDS
		4 LOADERS
		8 PUSHERS
		1 FORK
AUDIO	09.00	16 HANDS
		4 RUNNERS
VIDEO	10.00	12 HANDS
SET	10.00	ADD 8 HANDS
BACKLINE	12.00	4 HANDS
		W/ROBE ASSIST
SHOWCALL	17.00	4 HANDS
LOAD OUT	TBA	12 LOADERS
		56 HANDS
		8 PUSHERS
		24 RIGGERS
		3 FORKS

It may also be that additional pushers, loaders, and/or forklifts will be needed if the load out is tricky or time is tight. This will be dealt with in the advance.

RUNNERS

The PURCHASER agrees to provide the runners listed in the local crew calls. The vehicles they will use will be the three 15 passenger seat vans. All runners, must be English speaking, hold valid drivers' licenses, have the necessary insurance, and possess a thorough knowledge of the local area including relevant suppliers, stores, and outlets. All runners must carry cell phones. The catering runner should be in an estate car or similar.

If there are any restrictions (insurance or otherwise) that would prevent these runners from transporting ARTISTs or crew, the PURCHASER agrees to provide a professional ground transportation service for the use of the ARTIST production.

SPOTLIGHTS

The PURCHASER shall provide four (4) follow spots with English-speaking experienced operators. If the venue does not have these lights then the PURCHASER shall arrange for the rental and installation of the lights at the PURCHASER's cost.

POWER

All services are to be 3 phase 120V/208V 5 wire:

E-N voltage should be 0 volts

E-L voltage should be +/−120 volts

N-L voltage should be +/−120 volts

L-L voltage should be +/−208 volts

A	RIGGING	250 Amps	USR
B	LIGHTING	2 × 400 Amps	USR AND USL
C	VIDEO	400 Amps	USC
D	LASERS	100 Amps	USR
E	AUDIO	400 Amps	SR
F	SHORE POWER	60 Amps	

Should the venue not have the necessary power to support the production, the PURCHASER agrees to provide generator sets to supplement the venue power. These sets must be placed at a suitable distance so as not to interfere with the show and all cables necessary to provide the above power supplies shall be provided, installed, and made safe prior to the load in.

OFFICES

The PURCHASER agrees to provide the following rooms for offices. All rooms must be clean, well lit, heated, and air-conditioned.

a. Production Office

One large clean room with six 6′ trestle tables, two rolling comfortable office chairs and two large trash cans and two large recycling cans; one for paper and one for other recycling.

Our tour carries and Road WIFI touring internet/printing system that takes care of all our network needs, including WIFI, VOIP, and printers. We will need one IP address from the house network to create our own network, which is fully managed, bandwidth throttled and secure.

Specific needs:

One hard wire Ethernet connection in the production office that has

Download speed of 25 mbps or higher

Upload speed of 10 mbps or higher

No firewall blocking of SIP traffic (TCP or UDP) for voice

No WIFI spoofing (SSID or MAC)

No blocking of VPN tunnel traffic

As little routing as possible is preferred. We would prefer a straight pipe out.

b. Tour Management

One clean and comfortable room furnished with four 6′ trestle tables, three office chairs, and a two-seater couch.

c. Security Office

One clean and comfortable room furnished with two 6′ trestle tables and two office chairs.

d. Tour Accounting

One clean and comfortable room furnished with two 6′ trestle tables and one office chair.

e. Management

One clean and comfortable room furnished with four 6′ trestle tables, three office chairs and two-seater couches with a coffee table and floor lamps.

f. Crew

A suitable large room, comfortable and quiet. Chairs and couches and tables to suit the room's size. This room should have easy access to showers.

g. Wardrobe

A suitable work room located close to the washer/dryer hookup as well as the dressing rooms. This room should have private restroom facilities.

DRESSING ROOMS

a. Dressing Room #1

A clean, comfortable, and private dressing room for the ARTIST'S exclusive use, capable of being locked at all times. This room shall be dry, heated, and air conditioned. It must be well lit, and have the following furnishings and facilities.

Full-length mirror

Lounge seating for eight people

Private restrooms and showers

Two full couches

One love seat

Two end tables

One coffee table

Assorted rugs

Floor and table lamps

b. Dressing Room #2

A clean, comfortable, and private dressing room for the ARTIST'S exclusive use, capable of being locked at all times. This room shall be dry, heated, and air conditioned. It must be well lit, and have the following furnishings and facilities.

Full-length mirror

Lounge seating for eight people

Private restrooms and showers

Two full couches

One love seat

Two end tables

One coffee table

Assorted rugs

Floor and table lamps

c. Dressing Room #3

A clean, comfortable, and private dressing room for the ARTIST'S exclusive use, capable of being locked at all times. This room shall be dry, heated, and air conditioned. It must be well lit, and have the following furnishings and facilities.

Full-length mirror

Lounge seating for eight people

Private restrooms and showers

Two full couches

One love seat

Two end tables

One coffee table

Assorted rugs

Floor and table lamps

SHOWERS

The PURCHASER and the venue agree that the venue will be made available at least one hour prior to the load in time and at least one hour after the load out ends in order for the ARTIST'S crew to take showers.

If the venue does not have shower facilities, then the PURCHASER agrees to provide six shower rooms at nearby accommodation with transportation to and from the venue.

The PURCHASER agrees to provide 120 bath towels for the use of ARTIST'S production. These towels should be delivered to the production office prior to load in time.

WASHER/DRYER

The ARTIST is touring with a washer and dryer set up. These will need to be connected as soon as they come off the truck.

VIP

It may be that the ARTIST will be conducting a VIP event. If this is to happen, a representative of the ARTIST will be in touch during the advance to organise a suitable location for this event.

SPONSORSHIP

There are NO sponsors associated with this tour.

MISCELLANEOUS

The ARTIST production will require the following miscellaneous items.

a. Suitable covers for all cables and multicore runs

b. Two mops/buckets, two large brooms, and one vacuum cleaner

c. Five large SULO type trash cans to be placed around the stage

CAMERA POLICY

This will be thoroughly addressed in the security advance but to emphasise it here also. There is a strict NO CAMERA policy with this ARTIST. This includes house IMAG, ISO locked off cameras, local personnel's private cameras or smartphones or ANY other photography of the ARTIST or the ARTIST'S production.

Please contact us the ARTIST production manager if you do not understand any of this document.

THANKS FOR READING

THE PRODUCTION TEAM.

CHAPTER 11

Good Advice

I was unsure of what to call this chapter. 'No' is not a word that a successful artist is used to hearing. You work for these people and so are subordinate to them. The very notion that you should be ready to say 'no' as a first response may seem to be counter to the very basic dynamic of your relationship with your client. This is all true, but your job is not as simple as that. You are hired because of your experience with building and touring shows, so you must find ways to bring that experience to bear in all situations. I am not advocating that your default advice is negative but I am saying that you should be a realistic advisor.

I have often been called a direct person. I was brought up not to talk around corners but to say what I think. I know that in some jobs this might not be a particular help but in Production Management, I believe it is important. You can be a part of the difference between a show, a festival, or a tour being successful or not, so with that sort of responsibility it is important to always be very clear about what you think ... and be like that all the time ... (there is that consistency theme again).

Firstly, let's remember that this is a business and for it to succeed it needs to be profitable. There is no logic to airfreighting all your equipment to another continent for a show if the fee for the show is going to be entirely eaten by the cost of the freight. These are the decisions and problems that will make up a large part of your everyday.

Secondly, your client expects you to have this knowledge. Consider the different paths and careers in the business. Production Management is the top on one of those paths, so with that being known, you must understand that the manager, the tour manager, or other person in that client role may not have taken the same road that you did and therefore may have a different sort of experience. "Surely this is obvious?" I hear you say. Well not as obvious as you might think. As you grow in this career, you must 'collect' this knowledge. Learn what works, what is suitable and by extension what doesn't or isn't.

Let us take a 'fictitious' example to show the end result of the decision making process for two acts operating at the same level. Both acts with a fairly traditional rock set up. Neither would be an act that you would expect to have a huge show with over the top special effects or massive sets etc. Their fans were just into the music. The musicianship was at a very high level for both. Both acts headlining the same festival on different nights.

DOI: 10.4324/9781003231349-11

Both acts had been touring the European summer with a mix of arenas and headline festival appearances.

The first act carried the usual backline and a full monitor system with front of house (FOH) control. A lighting floor package was also included. It all fitted nicely into one 45′ trailer. The other act was carrying a full light show, a full video package plus the usual set and audio gear. They were in seven 45′ trailers. This example is not to get you to judge either situation. It is to point out that the decision making process that leads to the end result (a headline appearance at a festival in this case) should be a considered one. You are not the driver of this process in any way. The artist will deliver the show they want to. I am only asking that you understand that a very similar result (this time I am talking about the artist delivering the performance that their fans have paid for and want) for the fans can have two drastically different sets of economic decisions behind them.

> *I am also not saying that shows should not be big and spectacular. Not at all. We are in the business of entertainment and the expectations of the audience need to be addressed and satisfied if we expect them to continue to buy tickets. My point is that a good PM must understand the environment that she or he is asked to work in. Know what your client is wanting to produce and advise the best way to achieve it. It is not in your remit to stifle or judge. Some artists can deliver a brilliant show without a massive production, and for some the production is an integral part of the performance. Know that there are different paths to the same result.*

A good management organisation wants to make their client successful, and so they will try to do everything to achieve this. And the artist will be wanting to do the same thing obviously. It is rock and roll legend that in the 1970s and 1980s bands like Pink Floyd and Genesis maybe lost money touring because they wanted to produce such over the top and spectacular shows. Now I do not know if this is factual, BUT if you were lucky enough to have seen these shows, you were simply stunned by the scope and scale of the design. They set the bar early and they set the bar high, if you take into account WHEN they were produced.

I am so very lucky to have spent nearly two decades running a big touring festival. This gave me the opportunity to be involved with hundreds of different shows. To see what worked and what failed. To watch the frustration of a crew as they tried desperately to squeeze too much gear on to a stage that was too small, and also to hear the roar of 65,000 people as they showed their approval of a spectacular show. Then some years where I got to work as a local site coordinator with the big stadium shows of the early 1990s. Huge shows that showed what could be done when there was a big budget. This has not stopped. More and more, bigger and bigger. And now, as we run headlong into accelerating climate change, big but also sustainable. This is a new challenge.

I see a big part of this job of production manager as the adviser. And knowing when to say YES or NO is the very essence of this role. To counsel and assist the artist in the delivery of their art in the live forum.

C H A P T E R   1 2

The On Sale

The reason we do what we do. This is what makes the business successful or not. The artist hopes to do two things here.

1. To sell all the tickets

2. To put on a great show

If they do the first and then the second, then they will have a good chance of doing the first again, and so on.

THE SALE OF THE TICKETS

Selling tickets used to be quite a simple process. There was a hall or a theatre that could fit a certain number of people. The management did a deal with a promoter who bought the show. The show was advertised and then the tickets went on sale. People bought them and that was that. Today things are a little different.

Over the past few decades the internet has made the sale of tickets a more complex task. Patrons can view the seating plan and make selections based on their previous knowledge of the venue, the show, the artist, etc., or by reading the latest comments about the show on social media. Different levels of ticket price. VIP experiences, Gold sections, backstage tours, all on the market for the fans to buy. The world of ticketing is complex I am no expert in it, so will leave the details to others.

You might ask why there is a chapter on selling tickets in this book. Why should a production manager worry about the selling of tickets? The actual promotion of the show, the ticket prices, the on-sale date, the publicity, and everything else that is involved with the selling of a concert are not within the remit of the production manager, but the promoter needs to know *where* tickets can be sold in the venues the artist is performing. The sightlines, the stage placement, the size of the production are all factors that will have an impact here and so you are involved.

DOI: 10.4324/9781003231349-12

SIGHTLINES

The fairly obvious premise is that everyone who buys a ticket to the show should be able to see and hear it. Here you will do the balancing act of both ensuring that the show is produced as it is intended by the artist whilst maximising the sightlines. The promoter wants and needs to sell as many tickets as possible especially as it gets close to the point where they are in profit share. The artist feels similarly obviously but with a guarantee deal the financial pressure is lessened. The crew want all the bits and bobs for the full show so that they can do the job they are paid to do. Oftentimes it seems that some people on the crew think the lack of space, height, depth, etc., is someone else's problem. This single mindedness is something you will come across again and again. Time to put the blue helmet on and work on the necessary compromises. A guitar tech may well believe that every part of her or his 'world' must be in the exact same position relatively for every gig ... and yes they are correct to a certain extent. A lot of tech 'worlds' as we call them may have become over time as much about the comfort of the tech as the need of the artist. How will you know what to decide unless you understand how the tech in question works and what her or his duties during the show are ...? You won't, so you must gain this understanding by being the observer. If your path to this job included time behind a monitor desk or tuning guitars then you will have a decent understanding of the needs of the crew working in these roles. If not then time to observe ... but unless the circumstance is found to be a 'showstopper' then the sightlines should take precedence. By 'showstopper' I mean that the artist cannot perform unless things are a certain way ... think a particular array of monitor speakers, the exact positioning of a cab or some part of the artist rig. Some on the crew may try and sell you the 'this is a showstopper' line, and hopefully they are speaking truth and not just making things easier in their world. You will find out quickly which one is true.

SECONDARY MARKETS

If you 'sell out' in today's industry, you may not have actually delivered all the available tickets to the end users. That is, a portion of the inventory will be 'purchased' by bots, or secondary market ticket sellers. These entities will then seek to on-sell the tickets for an inflated price. This seems like scalping, right? Well it is exactly the same. Big Deal I hear someone say ... well let us examine an issue that has relevance for the artist, the promoter, and by extension, you.

The schedule and timing of the design and build of the show run according to the timeline that suits delivery of the show in time to rehearse and then to tour. The selling of the tickets and that timeline runs according to what works for that. It may be important to go on sale early to compete with rival tours or a festival. It may be important to time the on sale with the release of the new record. My point is that these two components are not usually in sync. What does this mean? As you read further, be aware that this is only relevant for arena and stadium shows where these issues of sightline are real problems.

Remember we have spoken about the fairly obvious need for all patrons who have purchased a ticket to have the ability to see and hear the performance? How far around the arena can you sell tickets? What seats are blocked by production? These questions need to be answered before you go on sale. But how do you answer these questions (and yes, it is you that must answer) if the on sale is before the show is fully understood and the design completed and approved? You cannot ... but it is a good idea to come as close as you can and here is why.

Recently I had a run of arena dates through various A markets. All of these shows were pretty much a shoe in to sell out. As there were a few issues with the design still to be resolved, instructions were issued to the promoters to sell to the 180 line. In Figure 12.1, you will see there are two green lines running across the arena at the downstage edge (DSE). The one that is flat across the downstage edge is what is called a 180 line and the other angled line is a 220 line. Obviously these numbers refer to the angle of the line in relation to the DSE. Have a look at the number of seats that are between the two lines.

We went on sale and everything sold out in hours. Great result. However, there was a problem which was not apparent until day of show.

As was normal in the schedule of the advance we came to understand the final design and then we could review the on sale maps with a view to releasing seats on the side past the 180 line. This was done and many hundreds of good seats on either side of the stage were put into the system for sale. Basically those between the 180 and the 220. A few hundred seats. Job done right?

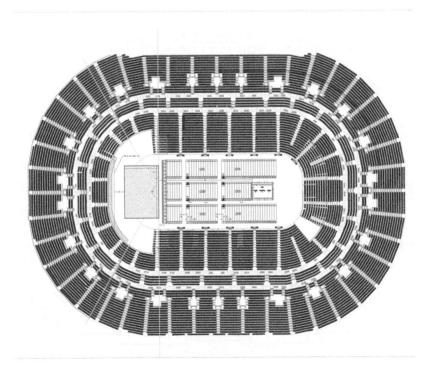

Figure 12.1 Arena seating plan

Well, not so fast. I arrived for load in on the day of show and was given the current sold map as is usual. The seats that we had released after the initial on-sale had not all sold. A few had but the majority remained unsold. This was puzzling as this act was in demand and always sold out. The local promoter said it was because of the loss of momentum. Maybe, but if you dig a little deeper there is another reason.

At the initial on-sale where the show had apparently sold out, several hundred of the best tickets had either been purchased in lots by BOTS or by representatives of the secondary markets. (Think Stub Hub, Via Gogo, etc.)

The result of this was:

1. The artist had sold all the tickets that they had made available at the initial on-sale.
2. The artist had 'sold out' BUT there were still tickets available for purchase on the secondary markets.

Advertising that a show has sold out will obviously slow ticket sales!

When we released those other tickets, we were instantly in competition with the secondary markets. These outlets had better tickets for sale than the artist did and so they sold out and the artist was left holding inventory.

How is this allowed you may well ask. Surely this is not legal. Well it is indeed a very murky area. I am only aware of one court case where this has been tested and the 'artist' lost the case.

How do you combat this?

Before we delve into this let me state that this problem is only really an issue for an act that will sell out. If ticket sales are average and not expected to sell 100 percent every show then this problem is less of a financial issue for the artist as it is for the promoter. But, if the opposite is true, as it was for the artist I was working for, then it is a real problem. There is a fight back however.

To sell to the 180 was always an easy way to get the show up on sale without causing any massive sightline issues. However, taking a longer look at it, it is not hard to find a load of seats that could very easily be put on sale day one. Even though the show design may not be final or even half way done, it is indeed a rare arena show that does not sell any seats on the sides. If you look at our image above you will see that many of these seats between the 180 and the 220 are in fact excellent seats, and with the production standards of today, any patron seated in these seats would be getting an excellent view and be able to hear wonderfully well.

It takes experience to be able to say confidently that a side seat will or won't have a full view, but you have to know what to aim at right? Be aware that these issues exist and when you find yourself in the position of knowing the show parameters before the on-sale, then work with the promoter (importantly through and under the supervision of the agent and management) to get every seat you can into the system for sale from day one.

Now we understand the goal, let us examine a few issues that will have an impact upon this. Firstly and most obviously the show itself. The placement of various components may in fact change once you are underway, and this may have a knock on effect on sightlines. An example of this might be the addition of a flown sidefill where previously it was stacked on the stage, or additional lighting or lasers on the stage deck that may impact the view of the lowest side seats. So the job continues. Finding seats, working on relocations. I always spend a good amount of time walking around the venue checking on the sightlines. This is so very important as the fundamental is that everyone who buys a ticket should have the full visual and aural experience and if they don't they must be informed prior by either having purchased an 'obstructed view' ticket for a reduced price, or they are relocated to a good seat.

CHAPTER 13

The Show

PART 1. THE DESIGN

How does an artist build a show? With the live show becoming the major income stream for musicians more and more effort is put into design. The designers of the show bring the concept or 'treatment' and over time this is fleshed out, thrashed out, and finally it becomes a design and the design becomes a series of drawings that then become construction drawings and finally the show is built. During this critical stage is the time to be involved and to bring the experience of the venues, the gear, the people, etc., to bear. Work with the designer or design team and be aware of every development. *This is not the time to see if you have talents in design, this is the time to watch and listen and to absorb all the data relevant to the 'how', 'how much', and 'how long' of the installation. Your ego is not required.*

There are many wonderful show designers in our industry. I have had the good fortune to have had some involvement on a few shows designed by some of these talented individuals. I have also trod the other road where the whole show design is driven by the lighting designer, working with the artist. Once again here in the design process there are the different paths to the final execution of a show.

Look at Figure 13.1 to see the 'render' or 'treatment' that is used to present to a client to show what the design will look like. As close to a model as you can get without making a model, and then that leads to the drawing (Figure 13.2). This drawing is of the same part of the show as the render and is only one of the many CAD drawings in the design that are needed to take this design past the concept stage and to the actual construction. Top or plan views, side views, and front views. Then the drawing is also broken down into the different components of set piece, video cube, etc., so these may be quantified and sent for costing.

I have been waiting for my current client's designer to return home so that the design process can commence. He has the ideas and I am merely there to guide and advise with regard to fitting the show in, integration with the other departments, and cost.

We will present this design when it is complete. It will get torn apart and analysed but hopefully will keep its integrity enough for me to get it built.

DOI: 10.4324/9781003231349-13

Figure 13.1 A 'render' of a show design concept. © Tobias Rylander

Throughout this process, the key people who have input to the design will have opinions and sometimes the discussions will be robust. It is best not to get emotionally connected to a particular design, and to watch that those on the 'crew' side of the discussion do not either. It is important to remember that this is an extension of the art. The primary of the art is obviously the music, and is an expression of the artist. This is a tricky area. For you and those with you on what is called the 'crew side' of the process this can be like walking in a minefield. I refer to the earlier chapter about knowing the environment you are in. The artist may be very sensitive about the work. There may have been issues with the writing of the music that you are not (and should not) be aware of.

Be the quiet one in the room. Learn what the intentions of the artist are. Then try to help them achieve those. You know that the management will be watching and they will be the ones to ask such questions as "How much is this going to cost?" or "Is this possible?" A considered response after research is much more useful than a glib "Of course" …. You are supposed to be the guide, the calm and unemotional one who offers the objective perspective. And don't worry that you will be perceived as negative or obstructive.

Take a moment to think of the recording process and how an artist will go over and over a phrase, a pattern, a riff, to get it just right. It is not acceptable that after all that focused work the live delivery of the art is let down by taking the easy option.

Now to go back to our current design proposal. The first concept was approved by the Artist and from there the designer turned the concept drawings (sometimes called

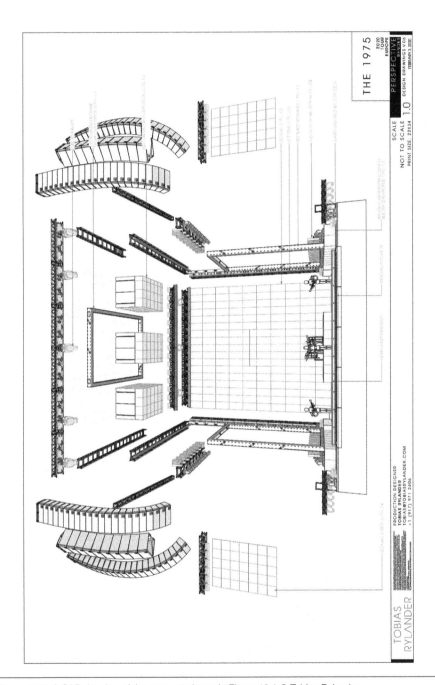

Figure 13.2 A CAD drawing of the concept shown in Figure 13.1 © Tobias Rylander

a treatment) into more substantial CAD drawings. The various components were identified and then it was time to take these various parts to the market for costing. Here again experience is key. Is this is design that has to be given to one vendor who can offer a turnkey solution? Is this something that can/should be broken up into segments and given to different specialists? These questions are the design teams to answer and your input will help. Here again you will be relying on good relationships with vendors that you have managed over time. It is a wise move to talk with the vendors about their lead time for a project prior to this point. In fact you should have had these lead time conversations as soon as you knew that a new design was in the works.

Time was our enemy as although we had submitted the concept to the client some months prior, we had only received the approval just now, which left two months until the start of the tour. You can see how we were now under pressure to deliver.

The bidding process involved the initial meeting with a description of the concept and a handing over of the various images, CAD drawings, animations, etc., followed by each vendor's responses and subsequent quotes. After a week or two (this should have been a longer process but remember we were under time constraints) we chose our vendor. Then after a few weeks the whole process stalled. We had a budget and it was being blown severely. This example is to show you how things do not always go to plan, even at a high level. With time running out, a decision needed to be made, and so after consulting with management, I pulled the pin and that version of the concept was binned. Now with almost no time, we needed to come up with a different version ... and fast.

Let's look at this. The artist had approved a concept, and tasked the creative team with producing it. The first design had fallen over due to cost (actually a huge mistake had been made by the vendor in the costing stage). BUT the concept still was the only thing we had to guide us and we therefore had to stay as close to it as we could. We went for an 'off the shelf' option that would deliver the result we were after; not in the way we originally wanted, but close.

You can see here how once again, the great god of TIME ruled our world. Good design always involves some compromise. I am not about to start an argument with the designers of the world, but for our business it is something I believe. This is art, but by its nature, it is not the unadulterated art of other mediums. This is a collective attempt to deliver art in this live medium having to deal with an ever-changing environment, so it ain't pure. It changes, it adapts, and gets better. One client used to tell me that the show design was an ongoing experiment, never really finished. Not something every artist or designer would necessarily agree with but a point well made to a tired production manager (PM) frustrated with how something was not working in rehearsals!

In summary, I am saying you need to be as out in front of this whole process as you can be. Be flexible, quiet, don't get emotionally attached, and always be ready for something to change or indeed, go wrong.

PART TWO. REHEARSALS

We have spoken about rehearsing. The band rehearses, and the crew need to as well. The show needs rehearsing, as well as the music. It is often very difficult to find a suitable place to do a full production rehearsal. It is quite usual to just book the first venue of the tour for some extra days prior to load in and get the production rehearsed. This is not always possible as the regular venues are usually busy, with other shows and of course sports. So the hunt is on for the B arena or other venue that is not so busy and within an easy overnight drive to first gig. In my experience it is important to schedule the rehearsals right up to the start of the tour. Having a large gap is not desirable as the artist needs to be 'show ready' ....

Obviously when you are starting out with a smaller act this whole subject will scale back. It might be that the band have rehearsed by themselves prior to the tour and have no need of this pre tour set up. But this is what does happen at the mid to high levels of touring.

Each artist may have a different 'way' of rehearsing. Is it a band only rehearsal in a studio or rehearsal room, for however long? Let's just use as an example an artist who likes to rehearse the band only for a period in a rehearsal studio. Every camp is different but the level of involvement here is something you need to assess. Obviously the band gear, possibly the monitor system, and maybe the front of house (FOH) control is needed; with the appropriate crew. You often see acts move into the band rehearsal with loads of crew; all the bells and whistles. Think about this as it will get really expensive really fast. If it is only a basic band backline setup with some risers then you probably don't need the stage manager (SM) or any carpenters. Keep it lean and your client will be happy to settle in and rehearse for the right amount of time to be really comfortable with the set they are playing. It might just be that your client likes to have the bells and whistles at rehearsals, so check and make sure you are on the right track. Obviously what I have just outlined is great for the musicians. What about the other components of the show? If there are dancers, or other performers, then their rehearsals will usually be looked after by others but if they are going to be required for a production rehearsal, then you need to be aware and ready to accommodate.

At some point the different components will have to come together for full rehearsals. This schedule should be worked out with all the stakeholders being very clear about the time they require, both for the time in studios on their own and the time together. Once this is agreed then make the bookings. I always put a day on the front and two on the end of a request to book so we don't get caught out if time becomes an issue. Do this so that the time is blocked for you but you only pay for what time you are there.

The full production rehearsal separate to the tour is an expensive luxury for a big act. If you know your artist will need time to get things right for your smaller and less luxurious tour, then, as stated above the obvious thing to do is get in early with the agent and see if the first venue on the tour is available for a day or two prior to the first show. Even if it is available for a couple of days in the week prior but busy the night before your show, it is often still worth it to book for these days as that load out and back in is a good rehearsal for the crew, and you are still rehearsing right up to the show for the artist which, as I have said, is a good thing. The next section deals with a full production rehearsal if you are fortunate enough to be in that position.

PART 3. PRODUCTION REHEARSALS

Today is the travel day to the city where we will be doing our production rehearsals. All the crew is flying in from home cities across the country and across the globe. If you and the coordinator have done your jobs, this day should go smoothly, and yes for me it has done. All crew are where they are supposed to be. It is always good to spend some time with everyone on the evening before the load in. There is excitement about what you are all about to do. Share in this, enjoy the time.

Our first day was a good one considering we were putting this together for the first time. I refer to the chapter on CAD. It is now that the work will pay off. Like in anything, good preparation pays dividends later.

The way you schedule the installation of a rehearsal load in is obviously a little different than for a show. However, it should not be a complete go slow. The visual departments (lighting, video, lasers, SFX, set, automation, etc.) are the ones that need the most time with a new show, obviously, but do not discount the import of having the complete production rehearse. It is often in the 'connections' between departments where the problems are found. A complete and detailed drawing will usually highlight these problems before and therefore allows them to be fixed (that truss is too long, that bit of set obstructs, etc.), but the real world is the final arbiter of what works and what can fit where.

I have said before it is in the drawings where you begin to get the essential in-depth knowledge of the show, but here is where this knowledge develops and grows ... in the problem solving as the show becomes more than a drawing or concept. Hopefully the designer is here at this stage too, not so much to solve the issues, although any help is good, but to ensure the integrity of the design is maintained. If not then this will come down to you (and any creative team worth their salt will be wanting to be a part of this). Remember you are all there to build and make this art delivery mechanism a reality for the artist. Short cuts and too much compromise need to be avoided. Stay true to what the artist is seeking to achieve and you will be doing your job. Do not be the PM who is constantly seeking changes to the design to make things 'easier'. Get used to the fact that if the show is a complex beast then it will test you and your team. You obviously should seek to change something if all involved agree that it is an impossible ask (in the circumstances of touring) but as I said, you are being paid to deliver a vision ... and sometimes it is hard. You rehearse, the crew gets better at the tasks set, and everyone can feel satisfied in the knowledge that they have delivered.

As you move closer and closer to the show, more and more pieces are available to be put into position in the big puzzle. Now, as the show is installed for the first time, as the problems present, and are solved, you should be taking notes on all of this. This is where you start to fill in the gaps in your advance. Here is where those outstanding questions on labour and trucks and weight and height and width, etc., are all answered.

The first day or two are spent getting the majority of the rigging, lighting, video, and the other visual components in. The flown part of the show is hung and up. Now the floor part of the show is installed and we can start to see the interconnections work. The stage and set, with its various floors, ramps, hydraulic lifts, stairs, etc., and with its add-on from lighting, video, and SFX. Same sort of deal with the flown rig, as in enough time to get it done but not too much time to be wasting money. If this is a brand new stage and/or set you should have representatives from the set builder there to assist with the install and basically teach the carpenters.

The visual department heads will want to be working on their looks, and beginning to plot the show. The overnights are critical here for this process, otherwise your schedule will blow out. Make certain when you book the rehearsal place that the overnights are accounted for and in your approved budget. Seems simple right, but this is a T that needs crossing and you would be surprised how often it is forgotten or assumed. This overnight work will continue right through usually as on a show of any size there are many looks and cues to get the show right.

As first the stage/set and then the other more peripheral components of the show are installed and tested, you are close and it is time to bring audio in. It may be that audio is not just the usual multiple arrays of speakers but has something different in the specification, such as an effect system or surround or some other whiz bang thingy. It may be that audio needs to use the flown lighting as a path for cabling some overhead system so you may have already had this department in and working. If there is audio out in the house and not just near the stage then you could dovetail their installation with the flown rig to save time and rigging costs. Consult, consult, consult, and consult some more with your vendors and don't be caught out.

The timeline progresses and you are now looking at the backline going in. You are close to actually having some time to rehearse the tech side of things. Now each department will be need their time to do this and that, the rig needs to be down at this time, lights out for this duration, a time alignment of the audio rig that seems to last an eternity, with backline complaining about all of it. This is your day now as you are close to having an artist onstage.

It is helpful for everyone during this time to have daily meetings with department heads to discuss what is working and more importantly what isn't. Let people speak in this forum as you will find that consensus is a better way forward. You may be the final yes or no but listen to experience and learn. These meetings will be essential to the rehearsals success and it is good to continue with them on the road. Giving your department heads some 'ownership' in the show is great for morale and a cohesive workplace.

Staying in touch with tour management throughout this time is obviously very important. It keeps her or him abreast of the issues so that they may properly schedule the arrival of the B and A parties into the rehearsal. See Figure 13.2 for the production rehearsal load.

When that day on your schedule arrives that has the artist in the venue, it is time to find some new energy. You have lived inside this build for the past days and overcome many problems to get to this point. Be aware that your client may well be seeing the 'show' for the first time. Reset yourself a little to make sure that you can take them through it the best way for them. And YES even now there will be changes to make. This can be a tricky time as anything major will cost and usually there is no time ... so this is another reminder of why you need to be keeping everyone across the progress of the build. Don't leave surprises for your client. Keep management and tour management informed of all the major issues that present and how they are dealt with.

Hopefully for you and the crew, the artist will be happy with the result and rehearsals can commence. There are too many permutations of this next stage to outline in this book, so I will just say that you should be always ready for change; always open to discussion, and keep in the forefront of your mind that your role is now one of support for the artist, the operators, and the show.

The above is basically a commentary on how a production rehearsal has actually taken place. As I said in the introduction, there is no one system for everyone. If you look into it you can see that there are some fundamentals which transfer to any situation, large or small. Whether we are managing a stadium production or a small theatre rig, the fundamentals are the same.

Give your crew, and, therefore, by extension your client, enough time to get a new show understood. Schedule the rehearsal installation in s similar way to a regular load in but space it out.

Communication is key between the departments to be sure that the 'connections' work.

Keep the design team and management involved in all the issues so that if big changes are needed they are aware of the reasons.

Figure 13.3 Production rehearsal load in photo by Nicolai Sabottka

PART 4. SHOW TIME

All the scheduling and planning is done. The advance was effective and it has all led to this time and place. The load in went according to the schedule and now you are in that pre sound check mode. Once again, there is no set method here. Some artists will sound check every day, and spend a good deal of time on stage, some will also sound check every day but are happy to run a song and jump off. Some will only need to check intermittently and some hardly ever. Find out how you client is with sound checks and schedule the time accordingly. Once again keep the tour manager (TM) appraised of how your day is going so if the check has to be pushed a bit the decision can be made before the artist is walking to the stage ... not a great look! If there is a support act then obviously they will be getting set up off stage during this time and waiting to jump on, get checked and make use of these last few minutes before doors.

Doors need to be opened on time. Simple. There are times where you will have to hold doors but unless you are struggling to be ready because of some major issue or other, you should be out on the floor of the arena or in the foyer of the theatre or club a few minutes before the advertised door opening time, with walk in music playing and in a calm state. For a larger indoor venue, this time is critical to get the audience in and seated. Like I said, unless you cannot avoid it, you want the show to start on time with the audience in and comfortable. Run the time forward and think about the ramifications of playing late or the terrible look of your client going onstage with the audience still filing in. You must be ahead of this and never play catch up. If you have to adjust the show times then make everyone aware when the decision is made. Obviously you cannot force people into their seats and the promoter will be the one doing everything she or he can to make this happen as they will be the ones who get the complaints and the requests for refunds. Talk to the promoter about what the experience is in the venue with crowds being late or on time. Most modern and well-run venues know how long it takes to get their audiences seated. Listen to this experience when you are planning.

Next, check with your venue security that they are ready for the house to be open. Make sure the stage is dark and no crew are doing any last-minute guitar checks or similar. Take some pride in the look of the whole space around the stage; clean and tidy and professional.

If all is well then let the promoter know you are good to open. I like this time the best in my day as I see the excited patrons coming into the venue and think over the day that we have had and what we have achieved as a crew. Time to take a minute off, clear the head for soon it will be ...

   ... Show time.

Here is a simple piece of advice. Wash your hands. Whether you are handling the band's in-ear molds or maybe helping with some costume or even passing a pair of drumsticks ... wash your hands first. Your day has been busy with crew, trucks, road cases, etc., and why take any risk that you might give one of your artists a cold or bug.

Understand that different people have different ways of preparing for their performance and may take different amounts of time to get to that moment of walking to the stage. If your office has done its job there will be day sheets posted around backstage and in dressing rooms giving the times for support act/s, changeover and the start time for your show, so then you need to work on a schedule of warning about time until show, time until stage, time until the walk, whatever it is … the point where the artist and supporting performers; dancers, or band start work. If you have dancers, or a complicated wardrobe and costume set up, you will need to give a lot more notice. Here you need to talk to the head of wardrobe and discuss what calls her or his department will need to be prepared and ready. Monitor this and adjust as necessary. As we have discussed, time is everything and you must be always thinking of the final note of the show, knowing what time that must be and working back from there to where you are.

You can see how this thought process continues in reverse from the show all the way back to the initial discussions about the show design and the tour routing. And if all the many hundreds of decisions are made with consideration and consultation, you should find yourself ready to walk the artist to the stage with time and in a calm state.

Now the moment where even after more than three decades of doing it, the hairs still go up on the back of my neck … "Go House Lights" … the crowd roars and the artist walks to the stage.

PART 5. THE LOAD OUT

Just everything in reverse right?

Although reasonably accurate, very much an oversimplification of what is an extremely important part of the show day. This is very much within the remit of the SM. He or she is in charge of this time. You are to support and assist. Some time prior to the stagehands filing in and the load out commencing, you must sit with the SM and go through the proposed labour schedule for the load out. Discuss what the truck loading will be (the same every night) and where the challenges are. Let the SM do her or his job now. It is simply bad management to hire someone and then try and do their job for them. If you lay out and make clear what you want prior to the tour or at least before the first load out then they can manage it from there.

On smaller tours, you might not have a SM and so the load out is down to you. But usually if the tour is that small it is logical to expect that the load out will be smaller, shorter, and less complicated. As a PM over the past few years I have done tours where it was one truck and I packed it myself every night with the driver (and loaders of course); where it was seven trucks and I packed my own cases and got out of the way of an extremely accomplished SM who had his system down: getting all trucks away in 1 hour and 35 minutes on average, and where it was 17 trucks and I looked after getting the hallway cases to the dressing room hallway truck and then got out of the way.

This last example was a tour where the rigging marks out happened at 5:00 AM and so obviously I was there at that time. It is not safe to work from that time until the end of a load out each show day, so I had the SM come in with the lighting call at 7:00 AM and then I would hit the bunk after the hallway cases were on the dock. This way we shared the long hours. Once again you can see that there is not a set in stone formula. Work with the SM to find the best way you can be useful to the load out and stick with it every night. I have not yet met a SM that does not think the load out is a time trial, so you can usually be assured that the time spent packing trucks will shrink as you go on. If you don't have a SM then it is down to you to ensure that this difficult time of the work day is done in an efficient and safe manner. Be aware of the hours that you and your crew rack up day after day and work to share the load when you can to make sure you are not pushing people too hard. Ensure that there are always enough stagehands to assist. Act in a professional manner. The days we tell stories about are gone and that is a good thing.

PART 6. PLAYING AT FESTIVALS

Changeover has started. The band before us on this stage is a biggish one and there is much gear to remove before we can push forward ....

Now is the time to

1. Give the band the 30-minute warning, or what has been agreed to either directly or through the TM, wardrobe or security/assistants ...
2. Final check with Promoter about curfew in case of an issue.
3. Make sure your radio battery is fresh.
4. Monitor the progress of the changeover.

On a lot of big festivals your dressing rooms are a long way from the stage. It is important to time the journey from the dressing rooms to the stage no matter how short the distance so you know when to walk the band ... allowing for intro and 'prayer' ....

The SM should give you a "we are good on the deck" call once the line check is complete and the stage is ready.

Inform the stage manager when you are walking/driving.

Calm and measured at all times. Build in a buffer so that you are able to deal with the little issues that arise and no one ends up running. I am not advocating changing the clocks (although I used to do that as a festival SM!) but work at this process. It will be different for a lot of shows ... so I always work it out early in the day ... the distance to the stage ... the state of play generally, anything that speaks to the amount of time needed to get the stage. Once you have factored all the issues, you can work out the time to walk/drive, and then you can work it back from there ... lock it in and then tell the key people. The SM, wardrobe department, security, the TM, etc., anyone that is involved. Usually security will need to have a say in how the artist gets into and about the venue, and that is good as it means they are doing their job, so involve them in your plans ... walk it together and come up with an agreed plan.

It is more important that the artist take the stage in a calm fashion and not disturb their preparations, than it is to have to cut a song to make a hard curfew if you have a technical problem.

Let's talk about the festival 'push back' and real estate negotiation.

The key stakeholders here are all looking to negotiate a good position for themselves. The festival SM has a big job coordinating all the different acts and all their gear on and off the stage. Each act has a job to do, or perform paid for by the promoter. The audience at a festival is not ALL just there for the headline acts even though there is a reason they are called the headline acts obviously. Festivals are where a lot of younger acts are showcased and this can lead to success and the obvious extension here is that they return as the headliner! I have watched this happen. Each act has needs and is represented by their crew in this 'negotiation'.

You may be the PM for one of the acts playing a way down the bill, and you usually get what you are given there ... working up the bill brings more real estate and more 'privileges'. But there are tricks to this game ... and the first thing to know is that if you put the effort in before the tour was even on the road and worked on developing and building a sensible festival show then your days at all the festivals you play are going to be a lot easier. Too many times have I seen a band playing early in the day bringing in (or trying to) too much gear. This does not serve the artist, the festival or anyone else well at all. As you (and your artist) are climbing the ladder of success, reputation matters, and at a festival, it is about ALL the acts. Save your large set pieces and massive floor packages for your solo shows. Or save them for when the act is headlining.

Figure 13.4 Get onstage on time, but most importantly, get OFFSTAGE on time.

Photograph: Author.

You are there loading in to a festival stage in the early morning, playing fourth down the bill and needing to decide on what show you are doing. If you have done your advance correctly and the roof and stage are both what the drawings said they would be, then the decision was already made and your crew know what they need to pull from the truck and where it goes. But sometimes things are not what they were supposed to be for various reasons … some reasonable and some not. Regardless, time is always against us and the decision to modify the show is down to you. There are times to defend your position and insist on changes but you must always look at the reality of any situation. How is everything else? Is this issue on stage the only issue or are you fighting battles in every department? Take a quick moment to bring it all together in your head. Even if you stand firm on this stage issue is it something that the festival can even fix? Are festival staff charging about trying to get done before gates or are they calm and in control? Was catering good and the dressing rooms; were they as expected? All these things will speak to your decision as to stand firm or adapt and move on. If you work on a compromise and it is successful, then you have shown your leadership; taught your crew and the locals something and earned your pay for that day. It is easy just to shout and demand … the real skill is in understanding that compromise is always possible and often the right path.

Respect is so important. Respect for the people you work with; from your immediate crew to the local stagehands, the caterers, security personnel walking a perimeter … everyone. You might be a touring PM, with much responsibility but all the people working on a festival site or in an arena are all working for one purpose … and it is not to make you happy … it is to ensure that the transaction between the artists and the audience is completed satisfactorily.

On a recent European festival run, the act I was working for were headlining one of the biggest festivals and so we had the usual fun time of the overnight load in. We were in eight trucks and were carrying the entire light show and video package. The start time was 3:00 AM and we could get it all done in five hours … pushed backed, zipped up, and out of the way for all the bands who were playing before us. I always start down at the stage to work out where we would set and to be there for my crew in case of questions that needed fast decisions. As our SM and I walked towards the dock, there was a weird sense of tension. All the locals looked both tired (der) and apprehensive … unusually so. We got on the deck and started to work things out. One of our crew cracked a joke, someone else joined in and there was this palpable sense of relief … I looked at our SM (wonderful chap, full of good humour) and he looked back quizzically. He called the local SM over and asked him what had just happened (because everyone had felt it). He told us that the locals had been yelled at for the past two days by the headliner from the previous night … it had not been a fun experience at all for any of them and they were hoping that we were different. This explained the apprehension and now we knew that, we turned it up a bit. We were an easygoing outfit but now we wanted to make the locals feel good about their role in our show, so the jokes and goodwill flowed!

I only have to refer to my section on morale. It is well known and documented how much better people work and interact at work if their morale is high. Your aim (not always achievable I know) should be to make sure everyone you work with leaves you smiling or at least satisfied that it was a rewarding experience. You want people to WANT to work with you and your team.

CHAPTER 14

Festival Production Management

This subject deserves its own book like many of the subjects we are dealing with. I am sure as time goes on someone will take that project on and develop suitable technical texts for students and those seeking a career in live music. For now, I will touch on some on the main points that should be part of good festival production manager's (PM) body of knowledge.

Festivals are completely different environment. The fundamentals may be the same. The crew, vendors, morale, etc., but the way you production manage a festival is often literally governed by the environment. Here you are in a constant state of reaction. In my experience one of the biggest failings many festivals have had over the years is in not allocating enough time to plan. Although there are many variables you cannot predict, you need to be as proactive as possible so when those changes happen, which they do, you are as prepared as you can be.

The old way of building a festival was quite organic. My experience of this was a time for great learning. Later you can read the case study of a terrible period in my festival life, but for now let's keep on with the basics of good festival production management.

In the biggest markets it is often the case that a festival promoter will employ a Production and Site management team that will go to all the festivals that are produced by the organisation and run each one using the same or similar formula. This works well, often ... BUT it is my view that the location of a festival is a vital part of what the festival should be about. You might think that this is obvious and already entrenched ... just think of a few of the well-known festivals, like Glastonbury, Coachella, Roskilde,

DOI: 10.4324/9781003231349-14

etc. So much of these festivals are about the location. Do some research into these and you will find local history that is entwined with the initial growth and subsequent success of the event.

Staying with this, I think it is important to recruit the local community in as many ways as you can when building a festival. And what is the first thing that the location provides to you? The venue. By extension, therefore, I advocate the employment of a local site team. Apart from the obvious local knowledge about the venue and surrounding areas, there is also the same level of knowledge about so many other essential factors; weather, traffic, to name but two, that can hurt if not understood and managed (or avoided).

My recipe for building this local team takes time and will have some pitfalls but you are there to create something longstanding … wouldn't any Festival promoter want to have an event with the prestige (and earnings) of Rock Werchter? So it is the long game that we are playing here. Yes this is book on Production management but it is important to understand the big picture in every environment you work.

It is my opinion that a degree of the success of the Big Day Out was due to the very fact that each town we played in was managed and run by a local team. These locals felt a good degree of ownership of the event and were very motivated as they knew the job was theirs.

Stepping sideways for a bit, the bean counters amongst you would have already worked out the significant savings to be had by having a local team, the site team who spend the most amount of time actually onsite, the ones who have the most number of meetings with local councils, and other authorities. No flights, No accommodation … winning already right?

Obviously these past few paragraphs have me stepping outside my job description. As a PM these decisions are not usually yours to make. You are sent to do a job of delivering the production aspect of a festival. Whether or not you are lucky enough to be involved with a festival that has strong local ties or you are flying in as part of an 'out of town' team, the job is there to do.

It is usual that you will have contact and involvement with the extra levels of middle management that exist on a festival. There will be separate departments on site, artist relations, ticketing, sponsorship management, and others. Your successful interaction with these departments is critical. Attend the meetings and do your part even if that part is the quiet person with much experience in the corner!

The most important of these other departments for you as the **PM** is the Site department headed up by the site coordinator (often called the site manager). This team is tasked with, for all intents and purposes, building the venue. The challenges presented by this range from the obvious issues like weather to the more complex like building stages on sand or grass. Access, or the lack thereof, is a big challenge and on some festivals sites that are difficult, much money is spent just to get a flat and accessible work area. The festival site manager is a breed apart. Usually no nonsense women and men, who, like touring crew, often have to do what would be considered impossible to the average person. A good site team can be the one difference between a festival succeeding or not and I am not talking about ticket sales or income. I am talking about wind, weather, and other erratic and uncontrollable factors that can be dealt with if the site team knows what they are doing.

If you are a budding PM looking to gain knowledge, then I can highly recommend getting some work on a site team. Build some fences, lay some road. You will learn a lot.

Swerving back into our lane, we need to find good stage managers for the different stages. The festival stage manager needs to be a good diplomat, ensuring that the interests of all the acts are looked after as well as is possible. If there is ever a good cop/bad cop situation needed to solve an issue then you as PM are ALWAYS the bad cop. Hopefully the different acts' PMs have all read the section on playing at festivals and so will be all smiles and 'let me help you'!!!

Apart from being the diplomat, the skills of the stage manager on a festival stage are almost identical to those of a touring stage manager. The load in on a festival stage is usually more drawn out, normally having a day (or two) to get the festival production installed before the show day. Depending on their tour schedule the headliners for the various stages will often load in either that day before also or on the overnight.

The size of the workload of a festival production office is not dissimilar to a tour production office. It is all about disseminating information. And that is the key. In my opinion, everyone needs to know everything (with the exception of the money side of the job). I use a drop box or similar cloud storage system to house all the relevant information on each act for the festival and all the festival information in a similar way for all the artists' production teams to absorb.

I am going to say once again how I disagree with the use of an online portal for the acts to do their festival advance through. It is a lazy way of ticking boxes and letting the stage managers sort the issues out on the day. I believe that festivals should be advanced in the correct manner; personally. I am also not a fan of having the stage manager take over the advance from the initial production contact. It is my belief that the production management team is there to completely advance with the act and then distribute the information to the stage managers.

I used to draw up a 'rider' for the festival which I would send to all the acts. This document would simply outline what the festival was going to provide from the stage drawings to the dressing room accommodations, but the technical back and forth was always still done in person. This online streamlining of the advance is removing that interaction which is, in my opinion, an important part of our job. It is where young PMs on both sides can learn a lot about the negotiations that are a part of our world. It is also an important time for them to build their professional network and you cannot do that with a portal.

As I have said, this business is about the people.

Let us return to the production management job on a festival.

There is an order to the business which is not unlike the touring PM's role.

1. Promoter decides on the line-up and programme.
2. You establish contact with the acts, usually via their agent.
3. Your advance work with the artists leads to the festival specification.

The technical specification of a festival is influenced by two main factors. Firstly the headlining acts (one for each stage) will want input into the design of the production on the relevant stage. Often on major festival the headline act will bring significant production to the event.

You are a part of a larger group of middle management staff so there will be meetings about everything; and I mean everything. I can recall meetings about meetings that had not happened!

The big questions of how many stages, precincts (food, services, art, etc.) will be decided in the site planning meetings and may well not have much to do with you. It is however important for you to understand the 'why' of site design as it impacts upon every department. I always tagged along for those site meetings when I could.

If we can stay with this topic for a bit. To my mind the fundamental that should drive this design phase is audience mobility. Crowd safety is (a whole book for itself) and should be the primary focus of any festival management team. So we place the components of the event in places that will not impede this movement.

This is not a time for assumptions or guesswork. You will need an accurate CAD of the site. You will need scale drawings of all the components that can be placed and the real-life issues will present themselves. We used to cut out the plan view drawings of the various components and then move them about the CAD quite like an old WWII battle map you see in the movies.

Why are you here in this meeting again? The production manager? Put simply, the issues found and decisions made at this stage can and will have a huge impact upon your show day and the show days of the stage managers and the artists, so get involved and listen. Let us look at a fictitious example.

The festival requires two large stages, one mid-size and two smaller ones to accommodate the acts that are booked to play. The positioning of these is coming into a sharp focus as apart from the two mega acts that are going to close the big stages, there is an act on the mid-size stage that will draw a very big crowd at the time they play. They could not be programmed for the big stages as they need to play in darkness and were not popular enough to take the second spot on the big stages. So we are looking at this issue not from a musical, technical, or artistic perspective. We are looking at how to allow enough of the audience to move to the mid-size stage in order to see this up and coming act. The question of whether it is smart to put this act up against the headliner is raised. With different demographics it is a smart play as the audience will be split at a pretty critical time of the show day. The younger (maybe hipsters or younger females for this scenario) will be happy to move away from the older rock crowd. This will thin the main field out when the younger and maybe less festival savvy are weary and quite possibly a little (or a lot) under the weather.

Now with this as a known, then the combat agencies (first aid, etc.) can also allocate their resources to suit the situation.

This is just something I made up but you can see how very important this process is. When you get into the reasoning behind sensible programming of festival stages you really begin to understand the whole audience welfare mission. Obviously the promoter or producer is doing the programming but good counsel based on sound reasoning is welcome or should be.

Staying with programming for a bit. There are a few things that a festival producer really wants a festival audience to do during the show day.

1. Enjoy their day enough to return the following year.

2. See all the bands and exhibits that they want to.

3. Move around the site as much as possible.

4. Eat, drink, stay hydrated, and use the amenities.

5. Spend money with the various concessions, market stalls, rides, etc.

We are some distance from production and technical right now but the whole landscape of the festival environment should be understood by the key staff for them to do their jobs well. You now understand the major drivers behind a producer's decision making. The festival is an excellent training ground for many of the disciplines offered in our business. I highly recommend that up and coming PMs spend a decent amount of time working in this environment, if they can.

CHAPTER 15

Time

Your most precious commodity. And the stage manager is the person most responsible for the direct management of it. The schedule, however, is yours to decide. The number of trucks, the number of crew, both touring and local, local labour numbers, etc. What was considered normal in the past went something like this?

06:00	Mark out (sometimes called the 'Chalk')
07:00	Rigging
08:00	Lighting and other flying depts …
09:00	Video
10:00	Audio
11:00	Set
12:00	Backline
16:00	Sound check
17:00	Dinner
19:00	Doors

This time-honoured schedule is not as usual as it once was.

Touring today you may well have a VIP or a Meet and Greet event as part of the day. These have become a very attractive income stream for artists. I will leave it for another to write the book on how the recording side of the business has shrunk to be a shadow of its former self, but the short story is that the live show is now the primary income source for artists in the modern market and anything that they can supplement this with is very welcome. Hence the rise of the added event. What this can mean for the production department is that now you need to be 'show ready' earlier than in the past. This 'event' may include some sort of special viewing of the sound check. So, if the sound check is now part of the show, you just lost hours! Your scheduling of the day, and the way the stage manager installs the show just got more difficult. The room for error that may have existed before is gone. Time always was your most precious commodity, and it just got more valuable.

What this says is that now it is even more critical to have a comprehensive understanding of every minute of every day of the tour and how it will work. Schedules within schedules if you like.

DOI: 10.4324/9781003231349-15

These days getting a run of shows together that works is becoming harder and harder as venues are so very busy; the arenas especially so during sports seasons. Whereas in the past you might have been able to get a pre-rig the afternoon before your show day, it is becoming increasingly more difficult for the aforementioned reasons. So, the dilemma here is that the bigger and more complex show needs to be built in less time. Think about a busy arena. It is a Friday night and the NBA have a basketball game on. You have a show the next night. No chance of getting a pre-rig and you cannot start until the building staff have done their changeover … court out and stage in. 4:00 AM is about the earliest you will be able to start actual work in an modern arena if they are swapping out overnight … maybe 3:00 AM for some marking up. You have to check this in the advance as if you cannot start early enough it will have an impact on the rest of the day. And so to the rigging call.

If we remember that the sound check has been sold as part of the VIP experience, and the venue had basketball in last night. It is 5:00 AM and so you have 11 hours total. There are 16 trucks waiting to come onto the docks. The mark out commences. Your rigger walks to the floor and seeks permission from the house to begin marking up … the game is afoot. If the advance was thorough and two way, and this venue is known, then everyone will know what is happening today. I will remind you again that good and sensible decisions made here at the mark out can have a huge effect on how the rest of the day (and the show) will go. Make your decisions. Decide if anything needs modifying. Consult if it is appropriate, but if you have already played out this scenario in your mind earlier, then it should be fairly simple and the crew will be happy to know that you are decisive. After this, it may be quite obvious that your presence on the floor is no longer required. (Remember the adage about having a dog and barking yourself?). So get yourself to the office!

Time to get a little controversial now. Over my time in this business the world of the rigging has gained a certain mystique. There is sometimes a understanding that the riggers just do things their way, and because the rest of us mortals aren't riggers and don't climb (or do we?), therefore we just don't understand. Don't fall for this. The time of your rigging call; those early hour/s can make or break the entire day. The local riggers are (usually) highly skilled, well-trained individuals who should know the roof that they work in and your riggers and the head local have mapped the entire rig in chalk on the floor. Now build the points and hang the rig in the correct order. On the run I just completed I had a complex and unusual audio build with multiple arrays hanging throughout the arena. My video team were a crack outfit so I made the decision to change the usual order of call times and bring audio in directly after lighting and before video … Now this perturbed the riggers, as they would normally rig the show in areas. Working their way from one beam or bay to the next and pulling whatever chain they moved over. BUT on a show with 124 points going in at 5:00 AM with a sold sound check this would leave no margin for error. So the rigging went like this:

1. Lighting over the stage as well as audio out in the house.

2. Audio at the stage.

3. Video wall on the upstage followed by side screen points.

The riggers had to move around the roof a lot more and there was at times a good deal of complaining, but we did get it done in a timely fashion.

The fundamental here is that however the load in is scheduled should be matched by what goes on in the roof.

I once had an audio crew chief on a tour who would convince the rigger to hang some audio points as they went around the stage lighting points ... when the audio call was not for another 90 minutes ... you have to watch this if you are to be efficient. Now the final word of caution on this. The way to be sure that your rigging is hung according to the load in schedule is to empower your tour rigger to make sure of it. Let the riggers talk rigging and just let them know what the show needs. It won't usually help to have you step into this discussion ... let the normal chains of communication remain. You are the last resort and you won't be talking to the head rigger, it will be with the venue manager or the promoter.

I have tried to think of a different word to describe how different departments seem to only think about their own issues, but 'selfish' is the only word that suits. And I am not being negative here. There is pride in getting the rig, whether it be lights, video, set, or other up and done fast. Each department wants to do a good job; they are representing their employer and nobody wants to let the client (which during the load in is you) down. So yes a certain amount of selfishness is a good thing for them. So the stage manager will monitor and keep everyone moving along ... occasionally borrowing from one to pay another, etc. ... but keeping the whole affair going forward.

The above once again is meant to stress upon you the importance of both empowering your crew to do their jobs with confidence, and also that you should work hard to have an intimate knowledge of the show that you in charge of. The goal here is the have a crew performing at the highest level comfortable knowing that you are at their back. With many others out to take the little time we are given to do the job, it is so important to build the team and the team's confidence.

If you know the show and you know your crew and you know the venues then you can work on the timing details, and drill into the schedule of the day changing it, shaping it, all to make it go smoothly, and ON TIME.

C H A P T E R 1 6

Labour

Too often we see shows built around the constraints placed upon them by the labour companies. The rates of pay, the minimum hours, and the union regulations. This is letting the tail wag the dog in my opinion. I believe that the show should be built in the most efficient and safe manner possible. There should be, above all, order. You cannot have departments falling over each other in an effort to get their job done.

There is a five-hour minimum call in Venue X. This means that each stage hand or other casual staff is paid for five hours minimum even though he or she may only be needed for three or four hours for example. Some unions have a longer minimum, some up to eight hours. The other thing to note is that on average after five hours of work a stagehand or rigger or other will have to be fed. Some countries will send the person away for a meal break, but in the major markets you will need to send them to tour catering.

This being given then the promoter or labour company may want you to bring on all the hands you will need for the build at the first call and then peel them off as they are done. Their logic for this is that it is the cheapest way to get the show built. To my mind, this can be counterproductive for a successful show build. The rules will dictate also that any hand who works past their minimum will then need to be fed. So, let's say you need 36 hands to build your show in total. If you follow their method, you will have 36 hands starting work on the first call, which is usually rigging and then lighting. You are not going to need 36 hands for lighting quite obviously so the pressure will be on to do more. They will tell you that you should unload all your trucks and fill the venue with gear and then bring on the other departments quickly to use the labour. This is a recipe for chaos, and where was the memo that put someone other than you and the stage manager in charge of building the show? Let us return to the load in.

My preferred method is a system of rolling calls. Critical to this system working is a thorough understanding of how the show builds. I tell my department heads that they have a certain number of hours to get their gear in and up. If they need more time then I break up their build into sections, each one has a call of hands. The key to this working is that when a call is up those hands are knocked (sent home). This way you avoid having to feed a whole bunch of casual staff which costs money. Table 16.1 is an example of how rolling calls look.

DOI: 10.4324/9781003231349-16

Table 16.1 Rolling call labour sheet medium size arena show

Markup		LX/RIG	Video	Audio	Backline	Floor LX	Second Video	Show Call	Load Out
Time	7:00 AM	8:00 AM	9:00 AM	10:00 AM	12:00 PM	2:00 PM	2:00 PM	TBD	10:30 PM
Runners		3							3
Head rigger	1	1							1
Rigger up		12							12
Rigger down		4							4
Crew chief		1							1
Stage hands		10	8	8	4	4	4	4	46
Pushers		8							8
Truck loaders		4							12
Fork lifts and drivers		2							2
FOH spot ops		0							0
Wardrobe assistants		1						1	1
Catering runner		1							
Electrician/house lights		1						1	1
TOTAL	1	48	8	8	4	4	4	6	91

You can see in this sheet that both lighting and video departments required a second call of labour to finish their work. For lighting it was for the floor lights that could not be put in place until the set was built. It was the same for the video department as their projectors could not be placed until the set and stage were complete. The lighting department got the flown rig completed in the five-hour call and then got a lunch break. Their first call of hands was knocked off and when the lighting crew returned from lunch there was a new call of four hands for them to finish off the job. Most importantly, the department worked to a plan. There were clear parameters, no chaos and no other departments running over the top of them.

This system minimises the number of local labour that you have to feed or let go and have return after a meal break. There is a saving here for the budget but also helps the caterers to know that each day they are going to have roughly the same number of hands to feed.

You can see from this sheet that with one set of loaders, only one truck can be unloaded at a time. Although you might think this will not go fast enough, it does for a show of this size. Obviously for a much larger show you would scale up, but I am going to assume that if you are managing a show that big you won't be a reader of mine! The other thing it helps is that you get to start in a calm way … concentrating on the rigging and lighting without throwing all the gear into the venue and having people tripping over each other. I have had crew chiefs come to me and say that this method has really helped them work in a safer and more consistent way and they definitely preferred rolling calls to the 'en masse' approach.

Leaving this for a minute, I want to talk about the young techs on your crew. So many shows will have them arrive at the venue to find all their gear already unloaded and out on the arena floor (I am staying with an arena size show for all of these examples as it is the easiest to explain these concepts.) This leaves out an important area of learning for them … the truck pack. Their job begins and ends with a closed truck either backing down to a dock or leaving a dock at the end of a load out. Crew need to understand their truck pack, how it all goes in the truck, how the weight is distributed, leading to how the truck rides. They will never learn this if not given the chance. The rolling call system lets them get involved in this very important part of their job.

Back to the load in, we are one hour into the second call (LX) and the lighting crew have had the stage and floor to themselves. The riggers have pulled most of the lighting chains to the roof. No one has gotten in the way asking for points, or claiming real estate. Now the loaders move to the next department's trucks … in the case of the call sheet above, it is video and the next call of hands arrives. By the time the truck/s are unloaded (if you have enough riggers) the lighting rigging will be finished and the video points close to it. And so on until you have installed the show, your crew has all had time for lunch and there are minimal hands still on helping with the smaller projects that will take you up to the sound check. Obviously some roofs are slower than others and this will make my perfect example slow down a bit but you should understand that the intention here is not to have departments running over the top of each other. Work to achieve this separation and you will see the benefits.

This system is scalable for any size show. The example in the above table was for an 8-trucks 60-point show doing arenas. Table 16.2 presents a scaled-up example for a 17-truck show with 110 points.

Table 16.2 Rolling call labour sheet large size arena show

Time	Rigging	LX	FX audio	Main audio	Set	Video	Backline	Show call	Load out
	5:00 AM	7:00 AM	7:00 AM	9:00 AM	10:00 AM	10:00 AM	12:00 PM	5:30 PM	10:30 PM
Runners									
Head rigger	1								1
Rigger up	24								24
Rigger down	8								8
Crew chief	1								1
Stage hands	8	18	8	12	8	12	4	4	64
Pushers	8	8							8
Truck loaders	4	4							12
Fork lifts and drivers	1	2							3
FOH spot ops	0	0							0
Wardrobe assistants				1					1
Catering runner				1					
Electrician/house lights		1						1	1
TOTAL	47	33	8	14	8	12	4	5	123

What is different here? The first thing you will notice is the earlier start time and the longer rigging call. The department that has the most differences from day to day is the rigging department. With each roof presenting a new set of challenges, the riggers need time to get a complex show worked out.

You can see that it would not work for a production manager that does not have an intimate knowledge of every aspect of the show. Why? Because it involves knowing the numbers that are needed exactly. The 'en masse' method allows for laziness. You may get advised by the house how many riggers you should have and the local tells you how many hands have been used in the past for shows of this size. Just accepting this well-intentioned advice is taking the easy option. You should know what it takes to build your show. Simple.

The next thing you will notice is the change in order of departments. The video department load in was put back to after the audio. This was done for the following reasons:

- The audio rig was unique in that in addition to the normal left and right arrays there was an effects audio system that was rigged out in the house, over the seats. This meant a difficult installation which needed much more time.
- The video crew on this tour was a crack outfit and they could easily get done coming in later.
- The video screens basically shut down behind the stage more than the width of the stage so having the other 'big' departments in before they 'shut the door' helped the whole load in.

This sort of decision is yours to make. In conjunction with your stage manager and the department heads of course.

As we move through all the different components and departments you should be seeing how, through you, they are all connected. From the very first conversations with the designers to this point in the middle of a load in ... every decision is linked. It is about weight, time, and numbers. It is not rocket science, rather it is just complex. One of the fundamental skills you must learn is this interconnection. You will be the only one of the Production who is across every department. Even the stage manager's remit ends at the top of the dressing room hallway. You must engage with each department from top to bottom. This is not a job where you can cruise along. You must be on your game every day.

And this is very true for labour management. You should be regularly reviewing the way the show is installed and removed. Talk with the stage manager and adapt the calls to suit the changes. After a short while you will find the groove and then you will have the satisfaction of watching your crew fly through their work. All of you will have felt the production hit its stride and morale will soar because of that. Shorter and stress-free load outs mean more sleep and more down time ... and that equals a happy crew so work hard to get to that point. Listen to your crew; work with the labour companies and venues to achieve the best possible result.

Vendors

Let us deal with the external relationships that you will have and must maintain. The various vendors, audio companies, trucking companies, lighting, video, staging, etc., all will be looking to keep a good relationship with your artist via you. Over the years you will develop professional relationships with many different companies and individuals. These should be looked after and worked on.

Let's us remember that, first and foremost, the actual relationship we are talking about exists between the vendor and the artist. After all, it is the artist who is paying the vendor. I have often seen this relationship confused by either the production manager or the vendor. An easy way never to get it wrong is just to always remember …. IT IS NOT YOUR MONEY!

The stages artists go through as they grow in stature/popularity involve basically moving from being small to being big. Like the artist, vendors too will chart a course from small to big. Obviously an owner of a company wants his or her venture to be successful. It is often their life's work. These facts are even more reason to keep your relationships healthy and without burden. Do not let them become clouded or complicated. Shoot straight. Ignore offers of kickbacks. Becoming financially involved with a vendor immediately prevents you from acting impartially and therefore in the best interests of your client.

Your job is to manage the relationship to best represent your client; the artist. Now comes the hard bit!

It is important to be mindful of the bigger picture when dealing with vendors. To understand their limitations and to know when to push them or to 'cut them a break' is a vital part of keeping a relationship strong. Your primary responsibility is to your client, with your end goal being to produce the best show possible every night. This being true, therefore, your decision as to who you advise for appointment to the various tenders offered for a tour is a vital part of the process of achieving that goal. There is an onus on you to keep yourself abreast of the various happenings in the industry. Who is doing well, who is buying who or what, what is the state of 'health' of the vendors you work with. These questions need constant monitoring. Get involved. Talk with other production professionals, attend conferences and trade shows. Not only will you gain the very necessary knowledge of what is new and what can be done but you will also keep yourself up to date on the 'state' of things. Let's stay with the technology side of it for a bit.

DOI: 10.4324/9781003231349-17

It is an essential part of your skillset to be up to date with what is being developed in the business. Not just the obvious things like new developments in audio systems, or new/better intelligent lighting, but also the smaller details of how a show can be built and designed. Look at what is being achieved at the top end. Not to copy or to send your client broke trying to build a show beyond their economic means, but to see what clever and new ways things are being done. It could be something simple like a smart way of packaging a set, a different approach to managing the space around the stage. There is much to be learned from the successes (and indeed the mistakes) of others. Quite frankly, once you have finished your study (and read this book!!) your only path of learning is from the business around you.

Sometimes just to listen is a task; especially for someone who is supposed to lead and direct but listen you should. I like to ask venue managers about shows that have gone through their venues. What worked, what was cool, and clever? What did not work? Because sometimes all the money and cool tricks can come to naught if they cannot be built or installed in a timely manner or if they cost a fortune in labour to build and pull down. So listen to different viewpoints.

Your department heads will also make it their business to know these things but no lighting director is going to be across the latest in audio, and so on. It is your role to be across it all and therefore be in a position to advise and direct when it comes to integrating all these departments to make up the total picture. Always this is done with an eye on the budget. What can be achieved is governed by what it costs. Now, there are the biggest stadium and arena shows out there and it may seem that money is not really an issue, but it always is. Even more important than that, your knowledge base will include the 'tips and tricks' you learn from others' experiences.

This is your career and you are developing with every show, every tour, and every advance. Years are needed to give you the skill set of a good production manager.

Transport and Freight

TRUCKING

On a small tour with one truck, there is always one big stress …. Will all the gear I have booked actually fit in the one truck I have in the budget? This issue is linked to the 'Good Advice' chapter. In a carefully managed small tour budget, the cost of a truck is a significant part of the overall tour cost. Knowing how much space each department will need is obviously critical. As I write this, I am going over this exact issue. I have a run of all the major festivals in Europe. The cost of one 45′ truck at this time for this route is 30,000 GBP. I have budget for one truck, and so I have spent a good deal of time with each department making sure that we are not over. And that means both 'over' in space and also weight.

You have read the preceding pages about what it takes to be a good production manager (PM). All well and good I hear you say, but I am a young sound or lighting or backline tech and that seems like a very long way off. Yes, you would be correct. How do you chart the course?

It is important to understand the whole show. From truck unloading to truck loading and everything in between.

Let's start with the truck.

I was lucky (although it did not feel like it at the time) to learn this at the beginning. I was doing small tours where we had one truck and we as a crew had the responsibility of making sure all the gear fitted in it. We learnt to pack properly. We had to, as there was not going to be another truck show up if all the gear did not fit. We packed high and tight. In those days in Australia, it was on us to get the truck packed every day, so we quickly learned all about the critical issues in trucking; volume and weight. One of us was the driver usually and the stagehands just did what we told them to do (if in fact there were any stagehands). As a driver you learned pretty quickly that the weight in the pack needed to be distributed suitably … more weight over the drive wheels and evenly distributed across the width.

DOI: 10.4324/9781003231349-18

Figure 18.1 Sometimes it just has to be high and tight ...

Photograph: Author.

So that is how an old campaigner like myself got to understand packing a truck. You should, at every opportunity, get to know the inside of a truck. If, when you are starting out, you do some work at a production supply company (vendor); it may be that you do get a lot of opportunities for this. If you do not have that opening, then when you are on a gig getting some work experience, see if they will have you at the dock helping with the trucks. In some strict union environments, this is simply not possible, but you will find a way to learn if you ask and offer. One thing about our business is the older more experienced heads are usually very willing to share their knowledge (as long as you can deal with a few old touring stories thrown in!!).

In the United States, any tour of size will have trucks that have 53′ long trailers. In Europe, they are usually 45′ trailers, in Australia, 45′ or 48′, and in the rest of the world, whatever you get ... but usually 40′ if there are trailers.

If you start out on a small tour with a single rigid truck or a single semi-trailer, then you are in the best place possible to learn these important basics. Even if you just have a van for the gear it is still the same thing relatively. The fundamental point here is that your need to understand the gear ... its' size, volume, and weight.

At the higher levels, you will be expected to know pretty quickly how many trucks you are going to need for your tour. Your vendors help you here. They will advise on the amount of space that their gear needs. Most of them have applications that will work it out accurately. Apart from actually fitting in the truck, the other key factor here is the weight. You cannot just fill up a truck and send it. You need to know the weight ... as the driver will be crossing weigh bridges and if the truck is overweight, it will be stopped and told to unload ... not something you ever want to happen.

Weight distribution is another factor. There should be good weight over the drive wheels (in the nose) to help the load travel in a stable fashion.

Pack the truck(s) the same every time. Help your drivers out here … just slamming things into the first truck at the dock is never a good recipe for a successful trucking situation. This goes back to the theory of doing the same thing at the same time every day. Trucks packed the same will weigh the same, drive the same, load and unload the same … same equals happy … oh yeah and same equals CONSISTENT!

Figure 18.2 Same pack every day … Here the driver is busy unloading wall by wall

Photograph: Author.

TOUR BUSES

I spoke of the need to book your buses as soon as you know that a run of shows is happening. Often you can hold the buses with knowing just the start and end cities but just as for the trucks, your bussing vendor will need to entire routing to determine, the double drive moves, borders, ferries, and so on. The permitted driving regulations are complex as with trucks, and in the United States you must provide hotel accommodation for the bus drivers on every stop on the tour. The task of getting the bus drivers to their hotels early in the morning is usually top of a good production coordinator's list. On a tightly scheduled tour, it is absolutely essential to get these fine people to their hotel as a matter of priority.

The wonderful individuals who drive us smoothly to our next destination as we get what sleep we can usually have a wealth of knowledge and, just as with the truck drivers, a young PM can learn an awful lot from the bus drivers.

The etiquette of bus travel is something that needs to be passed on, needs to be discovered. It is not for a book like this. The bus is home.

FREIGHT

Another extremely important relationship you must maintain is with your freight forwarder. Often also called customs agents, or freight agents, shippers, etc. Here there is the lazy method and the right method. The lazy method involves less planning and knowledge as you might expect, but the correct method is the one you should adopt (as you might expect).

The primary job for the freight forwarder is moving your gear across borders. Moving into Europe from the USA, for example. This involves two major tasks.

1. Actually moving the gear by air or sea or road.
2. Compiling the manifest, and preparing and managing the carnet.

CARNETS

A carnet is basically a passport for equipment. It is also a promise. A promise by the freight agent that the gear on the manifest (which is a list of the equipment attached to the carnet) will not stay permanently in the country which you are travelling into (that would be importation and there are taxes and duties that must be paid in that circumstance) but will leave the country with you as the tour continues. As the gear and its carnet move about the world, the carnet is stamped in and out of countries with the end goal being finally returned to where it started its journey.

Let us deal with the manifest. An efficient organisation that tours a lot will have the list of tour equipment (inventory) kept up to date and populated with all the correct information like serial numbers, dimensions, value, country of manufacture, weight, and volume. Table 18.1 presents a sample.

Now it may be that your client has not toured regularly or not toured in other countries or your predecessor was not very organised and you have to start this process from scratch or near to scratch. Firstly inform your vendors if you will be taking any of their gear across any borders (this may well be very obvious to them already) and let them know you will need manifests from them as soon as the gear is known. Then you will need a blank manifest sheet for your client's gear. Ask your freight agent if they have a template or a friendly PM might sling you one. Then start. When complete you will have a manifest for the freight moves ... obviously ... BUT just as the rigging plot and your understanding of it will teach you about every detail of the flown rigs, the manifest will give you a thorough picture of the clients gear. This is invaluable. So with this in mind, do not be lazy; rather make sure you have every item and every case listed correctly.

There are other very important reasons why you should be accurate and detailed when compiling your manifests. In order for a freight agent to become a licensed customs broker, and therefore be allowed to move your equipment across borders (which is just one of the jobs they can do); they must sit for and pass exams. They must also show financial stability, and satisfy 'good character' requirements. Usually the firm must also post various sureties and bonds to be able to operate and make declarations to customs. These bonds are held as guarantees covering the value of any duties or taxes that are, or could be owed.

This means that the good word of a customs broker has a lot riding on it. Your manifest must be accurate and have every detail that is required under customs law as your broker's (agent's) livelihood could well depend on it. Inaccurate declarations can lead to many issues (all of them negative); including seizures, penalties or fines, suspension of bond, revocation of license ... you are getting the picture. Maybe it is just a red flag for future shipments meaning delays and close inspections; but this can be extremely problematic for you as TIME is not something you ever have a lot of. SO GET IT RIGHT, and understand that there is a lot at stake. My crew know that if we have a border crossing coming I will be going about checking that they are aware and not carrying anything in their cases that is forbidden and also that their gear lists are up to date. Often products such as coffee, alcohol, tobacco, etc., are not allowed to be inside a shipment (think borders rules when you are travelling personally ... very similar) and so people need to be aware in time to make sure they comply. Wardrobe cases often have this sort of material inside so check in with the wardrobe dept in plenty of time so the artist can make a decision about anything they want to keep but cannot take. No one likes to be ambushed at the last minute.

SMALLER MOVES

On a tour where the trucking company has been contracted to provide trucks to the tour and they are yours for the duration, those are what we call tour dedicated trucks. But often you will have to move some gear from A to B that cannot be placed in tour dedicated trucks for various reasons, a few of which may be:

- There is no tour happening at this time.
- You are gathering all the gear for the tour in the starting city.
- The gear needs to go somewhere that is not part of the tour routing.
- It is extra gear or replacement gear coming to meet the tour.

So your freight forwarder will pick up the said gear and move it, by road or by air or sea, depending on the situation, the urgency, and the cost.

Here I am talking about the smaller moves, and the reasons for moving are above. Also here it is important for you to be fiscally responsible. The lazy way is to contact your freight forwarder in every circumstance and just have it air freighted to where it needs to be. But very often there are better ways. Talk to your trucking company. Maybe there is a part load going in the same direction that you can throw your gear on with. Maybe your broker knows of some other act looking to do something similar and you can share the pallet. If you are seen to be always taking the easy/lazy (and usually more expensive) option, then it is going to hurt your client's bank balance and your reputation. The upside of doing a thorough job is that you learn about the ins and outs of moving equipment around the world and you become a more valuable PM to your clients and to your crews.

Table 18.1 A sample manifest

2	CASE	MAKE	MODEL	DESCRIPTION	VALUE (USD)	WEIGHT (US lbs)	ORIGIN (Country)	D"	W"	H"	SERIAL #	CUBIC
G00.1		INVENTORY	VERSION 1.6	EUROPE RIG								
G00.2				A								
G00.4				B								
G00.6				UNIVERSAL								
G00.7												14352
G01.1	G1	A&S Case Co.	Pedal board case	CASE FOR PEDALBOARD	$800.00	60	US	23	48	13	none	
G01.2			custom	Pedal Board	$150.00		US				none	
G01.3												
G02.1	G2	Dragon Case Co.	22-space 19" rack	Splitter world	$300.00							
G02.2		Radial	JD7 instrument splitter	backup	$1,400.00						224587	
G02.3		Radial	Bigshot ABY		$100.00						933331	
G02.4												
G02.5		Korg	DTR-1	Spare rack tuner	$100.00							
G02.6		Radial	JD7 instrument splitter	main	$1,400.00						606773	
G02.7		Furman	Power Conditioner		$1,000.00							
G02.8												
G03.1	G3		Triple Amplifier case	Marshall amplifiers	$1,000.00	160	USA	34	44	24	41393-19	35904
G03.2		Marshall	Super Bass 100W	Guitar amplifier #1	$2,000.00		UK				5598H	
G03.4		Marshall	Super Bass 100W	Guitar amplifier #2	$2,000.00		UK				07999J	
G03.5		Marshall	Super Bass 100W	Guitar amplifier #3	$2,000.00						xxxxxH	
G03.6												
G04.1	G4	A&S Case Co.	Triple Amplifier Case	Diezel amplifiers	$600.00	170		34	44	24	41393-19	35904
G04.2		Diezel	VH-4	Guitar Amp - Main	$3,000.00		Germany				na	
G04.3		Diezel	VH-4	Guitar Amp - Center	$3,000.00		Germany				#030385	
G04.4		Diezel	VH4	Guitar Amp - Revolver	$3,000.00		Germany					
G04.5												
G05.1	G5	Encore Case Co.	Single 4x12 Case	4 x 12 Guitar Speaker	$200.00	160	USA	18	34	40	41393-19	24480
G05.2		Marshall	Speaker		$500.00		UK				953032851	
G05.3												
G06.1	G6	Encore Case Co.	Single 4x12 Case	4 x 12 Guitar Speaker	$200.00	172	USA	18	34	42	41393-19	25704
G06.2		Mesa Boogie	Speaker	4 x 12 Guitar Speaker	$500.00		USA				C2-691295	
G06.3												
G07.1	G7	Encore Case Co.				183	USA	18	34	42	41393-19	25704
G07.2		Mesa Boogie	Speaker	4 x 12 Guitar Speaker	$500.00		USA				C22086	

(Continued)

Table 18.1 A sample manifest (Continued)

2	CASE	MAKE	MODEL	DESCRIPTION	VALUE (USD)	WEIGHT (US lbs)	ORIGIN (Country)	D"	W"	H"	SERIAL #	CUBIC
G08.1	G8	Case co	Double Footpedal	2 x PK5 case	$500.00	85	USA	16	26	26		10816
G08.2		Roland	PK-5A	Midi foot controller pedals	$600.00		USA				ZZ66096	
G08.3		Roland	PK-5	Midi foot controller pedals	$600.00		USA				AM53655	
G08.4												
G09.1	G9	Jan-AI Case Co.	Custom	Case for Access Virus	$250.00	45	USA	19	27	9		4617
G09.2		Access	KORG	KORG KEYBOARD	$500.00		Germany					
G09.3												
G10.1	G10	Ascot Case Co.	Workbox	WORKBOX	$800.00	225	USA	30	29	50	none	43500
G10.2				misc tools								
G10.3												
G11.1	G11	A&S Case Co.	Guitar Vault	New 2017	$0.00	400	USA	44	24	63		66528
G11.2		Gibson	LES PAUL		$3,000.00		USA					
G11.3		Gibson	LES PAUL		$3,000.00		USA					
G11.4		Gibson	LES PAUL		$3,000.00		USA					
G11.5		Gibson	LES PAUL		$3,000.00		USA					
G11.6		FENDER	STRATOCASTER		$3,000.00		USA					
G11.7		FENDER	STRATOCASTER		$3,000.00		USA					
G11.8		FENDER	STRATOCASTER		$3,000.00		USA					
G11.9												
G12.1	G12	A&S Case Co.	Trunk	Offstage trunk			US	27	51	37		50949
G12.2			supplies and backups									
G12.3												
G12.4		Roland	Cube-60D	Practice amp	$300.00						AT 26528	
G12.5												
G14.1	G14		Bullhorn case	3 MJK megaphones								
G14.2		Radio Shack	?	Megaphone	$150.00							
G14.3												
G17.1	G17	Jan-AI Case	Head Case (single)	Guitar amplifier flight case	$700.00	85	US	14	33	15	none	6930
G17.2				FOR RETURN PALLET								
G17.3												
G18.1	G18		Guitar trunk	LP-1 & LP-2 guitar trunk VIP		163		25	45	27		30375
G18.2												
G18.3		Roland	VK-8M	Drawbar module			Japan				ZT42483	
G18.4		Gibson	Guitar case	Guitar case (11lbs)	$150.00	25	Canada	16	44	5	none	

(Continued)

Table 18.1 A sample manifest (Continued)

2	CASE	MAKE	MODEL	DESCRIPTION	VALUE (USD)	WEIGHT (US lbs)	ORIGIN (Country)	D"	W"	H"	SERIAL #	CUBIC
G19.1	G19	Pelican	1720	flight case (19lbs)	$230.00	~35 lbs total		16	45	6	none	4320
G19.2		Access	YAMAHA	Desktop synth module	$450.00		JAPAN				D19901295	
G19.3		Access	YAMAHA	Desktop synth module #2	$450.00		JAPAN				D19901337	
G19.4												
G25.1	G25	A&S Case Co.	Single 4x12 case	Marshall 4x12 cab case	$300.00	160		17	33	36	13651-10	21318
G25.2		Marshall	1960A	Marshall 4x12 backup	$750.00						95013046	
G25.3												
G26.1	G26		Cab case	Single Mesa 4x12		173		17	33	42		23562
G26.2		Meas Boogie	4x12 4FB	4 x 12 straight cab backup	$500.00		USA				C2-63902	
G26.3												
G27.1	G27	A&S Case Co.	Tall 4x12 case	Mesa 4x12 angled cab backup	$300.00	160		17	33	42	13651-10	23562
G27.2		Mesa/Boogie	4x12 4FB		$750.00						C2-53922	
G27.3												
G29.1	G29	Jan-Al Case Co.	Custom	Case for Access Virus	$250.00	45	USA	19	27	9		4617
G29.2		Access	KORG	KORG KEYBOARD	$500.00		Germany					
G29.3												
LP1.1		Encore Case Co	Single Les Paul Case	FOR RETURN PALLET	$250.00						none	
LP1.2												
LP1.3												
LP2.1		Encore Case Co	Single Les Paul Case	FOR RETURN PALLET	$250.00						none	
LP2.2												
LP2.3												
G66.1	G66		Stage trunk		$100.00							
G66.2			Keyboard stands		$100.00							
G66.3			Footpedals		$100.00						TOTAL CUBIC	#REF!
G66.4												
			TOTAL VALUE		$5,280.00							
			PIECE COUNT		8.							
			TOTAL WEIGHT		538							

(Continued)

CHAPTER 19

CAD

The days are long gone where you would find the LD with his or her collection of plastic templates for the various components of the light show, carefully ruling and drawing the new plot. CAD came along in the early 1990s and is now an extremely important tool for all industry professionals.

I have one piece of advice here. Do a course and learn it. Get good at it. End of lesson.

I am not an expert drawer in CAD (or Vectorworks which is the program I use currently) but I am good enough to be able to use it for this one purpose; to gain the most detailed knowledge of the show. By working on and with the various plots; rigging, lights, video, audio, set, and stage plans I get to understand the show. I know the weight of it, the length of it, and the height of it. And from this knowledge I am in the best position to answer the important questions for my client and the promoters of the shows.

Can the show fit in the venues the agent is booking?

What are the sightline issues if any?

How much will it cost to load in and load out?

How long will it take to load in and then out which leads to …?

How far apart can the cities we play in be?

On a big show, it is true you will probably be touring a rigger or two or three. There is a stage manager and carpenters, lighting, SFX, video, audio, backline, etc.; all employed to have an intimate knowledge of their part of the show. Each department has its responsibilities. On the road, there are three who cross over all; yourself, stage management, and rigging. And it usually only you who will have been there from the initial concept discussions about the show. Unless of course you have the luxury of the designer being out there with you. It may well be that the designer is on the crew … quite often the Lighting director. This is a good thing as you can confer with the person whose concept the show is and that way make adjustments that will not impact upon that.

If you look at Figure 19.1 you can see the detail in just this one section of one layer of the overall drawing. This is the rigging plot, and each point is both labelled and then given coordinates in feet and inches from the rigging origin. So much can be learned from this information about how the show literally bolts together. When it comes to the advance you overlay this plot onto a correctly scaled drawing of the venue and you can

DOI: 10.4324/9781003231349-19

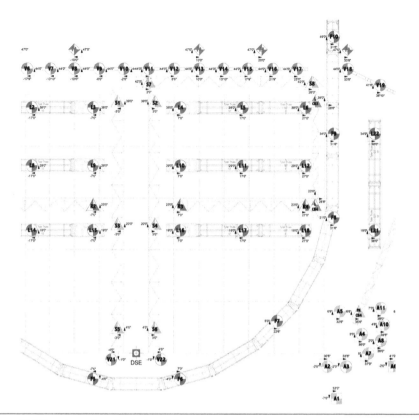

Figure 19.1 Sample section of a rigging plot

determine if it fits width and length ways (see Figure 19.2). In a front and side view of the overlay you can determine height, and with a calculator and the head local rigger or venue engineer you can determine if the weight if ok.

So CAD is an excellent way you can get to understand the show before you install it for the first time. The back and forth with the designer and the client is what you need to be at least aware of in the early stages. Look carefully at all the drawings ... and know them well so that you can do your job, as the design progresses.

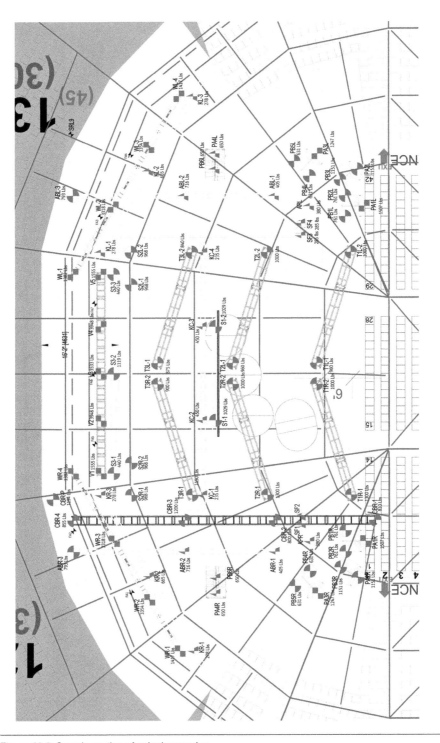

Figure 19.2 Sample section of a rigging overlay

CHAPTER   20

January 2001

We had a tiny team in the first years of the Big Day Out festival. We all helped out with everything and it grew organically. People and departments were gradually added but only when we really needed them. From 1992 to 1997 it was pretty chaotic, but it just worked. Then we had a year off in 1998 and when we returned in 1999, we started to get serious.

Then, in 2000, the Red Hot Chilli Peppers were headlining and we received a warning, if you like ... a shot across our bow. There was an incident at the Sydney show. We had a crowd collapse down the front and it was looking tricky. We went into our show stop, which was fairly rudimentary, but we were fortunate enough to have Anthony Keidis on stage and he was quite simply, incredible. He talked the crowd into calm. We got the kids up who had gone down, and we got out of it with a few minor scrapes. At the height of the incident, the senior police officer came to me, asking what we should do ... that stuck with me. The police did not know how to deal with this ... something needed to be done. In March of that year, the event employed a safety expert to start work with me on a manual ... a plan for when the shit hits the fan. Later that year nine patrons tragically died at the Roskilde festival in Denmark. It seemed we were on the right track.

The ideas we discussed in those months were many and varied. We talked about rescue techniques. We talked about barrier design. We look at pressure and crowd behaviour. We asked the question. How long do we have if someone is being crushed? FUCK I was a roadie ... what did I know about this stuff? But we wrote and planned, consulted and discussed, and planned on and on. A good thing we did because the next year, a tragedy occurred at one of our shows.

It was January 2001. All the wrong ingredients were present, and I cannot properly describe the awful feeling that was apparent in our audiences that year. The mood was aggressive and expectant. The behaviour of the some of the patrons had gone to a new level of what was basically uncaring. The number of confrontations between security and the audience was up, way up.

Our new policies on crowd safety included having face to face meetings with the acts to discuss the procedures in case of an incident. We had always believed that the ideal first point of contact with the audience in a situation is through the front person as he or she already has the full attention of the audience and let's face it they are here to see

DOI: 10.4324/9781003231349-20

their stars and are therefore much more likely to respond to them. We had this theory confirmed by Mr. Keidis the previous January.

The tour had been having issues from the start. I do not want to go into the details of this at all as it is not why I am writing about this time. I simply want to show how in the festival world things can change, change dramatically and extremely quickly. They certainly did for me that January.

At the first show on the tour in Auckland we had faced problems. A small but dangerous crowd collapse that did not produce any serious casualties due to the magnificent work of the security team. Next city was the Goldcoast and thankfully the show went without any incidents. Then it was onto Sydney and at about 9:15 that show night, this old sound guy from the 1980s found himself carrying an unconscious girl from the pit and into the First Aid post. This girl was called Jessica and she was a bright young 15-year-old who loved music. Her subsequent tragic death from the injuries she had sustained in that crowd collapse and the following police and Work Cover investigations culminating in a coronial inquest triggered much change in the Australian music industry.

The media were in full cry as were the 'experts'. This was a dreadful time and I cannot begin to imagine how hard life was for Jessica's parents. At the inquest, I spent three long days in the witness box with six different barristers all going for broke. I didn't sign up for this I remember thinking. This wasn't the Music industry that I knew. For me things had changed forever.

So, we used to put gigs on, book acts, build stages, install sound and lights, and now we had to learn a new set of skills. Our roles and responsibilities were different. A civil case followed the inquest and the responsibility (or blame) was apportioned by the court during the settlement. I was told that the guy or girl in my position of production manager had an equal amount of responsibility with the Promoter at 40 percent each. The security firm would take 10 percent as would the act. This was startling news.

Long meetings were had about how to move forward. A new barrier system was designed. The event was given a rating much like the cinemas, in an effort to appeal to parents about how young children should not attend. Many new rules and systems were introduced. The existing event surveillance system was upgraded to one with state of the art full site coverage. Safety announcements were played between each act, and live safety announcements were made throughout the day. The touring medical team was bolstered.

They were some of the changes in the show. There were also changes in the preparation of the show. The paperwork was increasing exponentially. Contractor control systems, risk assessments, Job Safety Analyses, insurance, inductions, and work cards. We engaged with the combat agencies of police and medical and conducted tabletop exercises. So, much more to think about and get done. Did all this make us better at what we did? Did all this make things safer? I looked and saw a different event. It was now a slick, vest wearing, sign carrying, risk assessing, and bureaucratic machine. Health and Safety was the theme. We were all about Health and Safety. I looked and believed that we would be doing well if we could get through all the new procedures, and we might even still be able to put a band or two on a stage, once we had negotiated to not have a hand rail across the stage front! All this new policy and procedure meant that we had to continually monitor and review it like never before. My job completely changed from then on. I used to deal almost exclusively with technical issues and logistics, and from then on added to that were all the issues of crowd management and safety. A new department called 'Show Management' was set up between Production and Security, which saw me and my security department counterpart walking the site all show day monitoring the crowd.

This example of festival life may seem rare, but events in the last few years would say no. Things that need to be looked at discussed, analysed and reviewed are many and varied and now include extreme events, critical incidents, active shooter incidents, and more.

I believe that you dear reader will more than likely NOT find yourself in a situation like the one I have described. I sure hope not anyway. I have written about this simply to point out that there is always a big picture to consider. The things that we do and plan can have an effect on areas that we might not have at first considered. Be aware of your environment, be aware of the people around you. Keep your head up and eyes open.

CHAPTER 21

Security

Firstly let me state that to adequately cover the roles of the security director, the venue security manager, and the close personal security it needs more space and detail than I have here. More importantly I am not a security expert and so will only give a brief overview of how Security interconnects with the Production department.

Security in live music started out when popular music became TOO popular and artists needed protection from overzealous fans. Looking back on those days; simple times where the biggest threat to an artist was probably from super fans or others trying to get too close. In today's difficult world, our industry seems now to be a target of nasty people, even terrorists who see a large gathering of people as a perfect target for them to use to demonstrate their problems and issues with society.

On today's regular arena tour, you are going to have a venue security manager, possibly a security person in charge of the Critical Incident Procedure as well as the close personal security persons who will be directly responsible for the personal well-being of the artists/s.

On small tours through theatres or clubs with a smaller entourage it is often the case that the venue security role will be yours in conjunction with the venue management local security head and the promoter rep. There may well be a close personal security person travelling with the artist, but at the gig in this case you are on your own. To deal with this, I encourage you to learn the basics and consult with an experienced venue security person in order to be able to manage the accreditation and the security briefing for the venue and promoter. The critical thing here as a production manager (PM) is not to insert yourself too far into this department as there are liability issues here for an inexperienced and unlicensed operator (you). You can however, distribute passes, and inform the local security about the show … how long it is, what the style of music is, whether moshing or crowd surfing or any other crowd behaviours have been a part of the shows previously. I will stress again here that you should be dealing with questions about what has happened and avoid giving opinions about what might occur. This is for the security professional, not a PM who is basically 'filling in' on the security job. The policy on photographers is another area that should be discussed and understood as many artists can be sensitive in this area.

DOI: 10.4324/9781003231349-21

VENUE SECURITY

This member of the touring staff has a big job. Firstly the production, publication, and dissemination of the security rider. Then, in the advance, he or she will be speaking directly with the promoter's security staff as well as the venue's. The rider will include a roster of expected security staffing. The protocols that are agreed to be acceptable for the artist will be discussed and finely tuned to suit the performance. From this the security costs can be added to the overall budget. This may go through you or the tour manager but more usually directly from the security department to the accountant or business management.

The coordination and distribution and ongoing management of tour accreditation is a large part of this person's role. Any tour needs to know who is backstage or in any other secure areas, and the usual method of achieving this is to issue accreditation. The immediate touring staff will usually have what we call an all access pass that will allow them to be anywhere they need to be. Then you will have different levels of other pass that allows non-essential personnel, local workers, photographers, guests to access the areas where they are allowed to be. It is all about identification.

What can you do to support this department? Security is one of the departments that will truly benefit from receiving as much information as you have. It is true that the security director will do his or her own advance with the venue and the detail of this is not within your remit. However, there are areas where you will crossover. The allocation of the different venue rooms as offices, dressing rooms, etc. Yourself, the coordinator, venue security, wardrobe head, promoter rep, and a venue rep will go through the entire backstage to assign the various available rooms to the different needs of the tour. There are some fundamentals in the world of security that may have the venue person pushing for a particular backstage/corridor layout. Don't be obstructive here as they are trying to make the venue secure for the client and for you and the crew. Of course there is always room for debate; for example, the wardrobe department may have particular room needs for the client also, so encourage the debate and push people to justify the position they take. Don't be that PM who demands a certain room for an office simply because 'that is how it has always been'. Be ready to adapt.

I think if you asked a lot of venue security people what they would like the PM to do to assist them in their job, they might answer 'Stay out of the way'. Joking aside, I do agree to some extent. But there is an interconnection between this department and yours just like the other departments. It is important to establish excellent communication from the outset. Oftentimes the security team is in adversarial or difficult situations in their job so be supportive and flexible in your relationship. Involve them in the things that will affect them. I have described earlier how security will want to have input into how the artist moves from dressing room to stage. Listen to their input and work with them and the stage manager to get it right. It is pretty embarrassing for this one thing to fuck up, because when it does, it is show time and everyone is in a heightened state. Don't be the one standing at the spot you thought was agreed upon, make sure that everyone is aware of what is decided and if things change (which they often do) make sure everyone is aware.

I have had clients that want to be met by their PM upon their arrival to the venue. They want to discuss the show and impart their wisdom to you. I also have had clients that just want to move in quietly with their security and the venue person and have no need of your input. Find out from the security team what the requirements are if your relationship does not extend to the artist and, if it does, then let security know what the artist is asking of you. Remember to communicate effectively. Avoid ego driven situations. Get things discussed before the venue goes into lock down and the security staff are heads down, prime directive firmly in their minds ... not a great time to chat.

ARTIST SECURITY

Sometimes called close personal, these fine people report to the security director. They will have their own schedules within the overall. Wherever their client needs or wishes to be, this person will be the one to escort them there and back. There is not a lot for you to do here (apart from not get in the way!) but if you take the relationship from their perspective, this may change. A friendly chat about how the production office is there to support everyone may be very helpful.

In conclusion, I advise you to open the communication with your client's security director early on and see where the two of you can support each other. Always include security in your information distribution lists.

The Economics of Touring

Firstly it must be very clear that this is a business. It is not like many others in the way it is structured but the fundamental premise is still there. It needs to be profitable for it to be sustainable. The production manager (PM) has a certain amount of input into this and the responsibility should be taken seriously.

One important point that sometimes gets lost in the world of production management is this. All the money comes from the same pot. Yes, the agent thrashes out a deal with the buyer or promoter and each party negotiates to see the best outcome for themselves. There is a whole book written on this topic and as we are dealing with Production Management, I will simply point you to it.[1]

We may not be involved in this deal making, but we should be aware of how it works and make sure that the decisions we do make are based on sound economics, not just for the artist but for the show. As in all economics for a model to be sustainable, the parties to the transaction must leave it satisfied. More simply, everyone should be making money and they will return to do it again.

Let's start at the beginning though.

RELATIONSHIPS

The artist has a number of very important business relationships. The first and most important to their financial success is with a manager, or management company.

The manager is the entity who is between the artist and the world, if you will. Briefly the manager makes all the business decisions in consult with the artist and directs all other parties. They will negotiate all deals with labels, work with agents on deals with promoters, and guide the artist on their career. A manager will usually retain a business manager on behalf of the artist. This entity looks after the money. All income goes to

DOI: 10.4324/9781003231349-22

the business manager to be distributed once all obligations are met. The business manager will manage/control the budgets ... all the budgets. The business manager will look after the bank accounts, pay the staff, pay all vendors, ensure all tax obligations are met, EVERYTHING. For a tour the business manager will work with the tour management (that's you, the TM and the accountant if you have one) to ensure that the tour is budgeted properly and often time you will submit your budget directly to the business manager. Like the other important relationships you have in this job, this one with business management is vital so stay communicative and yes ... you guessed it; consistent.

The manager will have a relationship with an agent or with an agency. The agent's job is to find the gigs. All the gigs everywhere the artist has a market and if the market somewhere is weak, then a skilful agent will get the artist exposure there to get more gigs and therefore income. A salesperson, if you like.

The agent negotiates the deals for the shows. Works with the buyer and promoter to get the engagement to contract. The agent is an extremely important part of the chain, and I like to make sure that my relationship with the agent is a good one. A forward thinking agent will let you have a look at a proposed routing to see if there are any logistical issues that should impact the run of dates. The size of the venues is a topic that should also be discussed with regard to the size of the show. There is not much point in paying for and carting around tonnes of gear for a show that doesn't fit in the venues that were booked. Other issues are timing/routing related; for example, touring in Europe with shows in Scandinavia will involve ferry crossings. These add time to any run and might impact upon the ability to get between shows in one overnight run. This is just one example. Also some border crossings are tricky and require more time as another example.

An experienced agent will know about a lot, if not all of these issues, but I find in this business it is the more experienced and professional people (in this case, agents) who will still consult with others to make sure of their planning decisions.

Let's now look at the cost to the artist for these services from the manager, business manager, and agent.

A manager will typically take 15 percent of all income. A business manager will typically take 5 percent of everything that passes through their business. The agent will typically take 10 percent of the deals they successfully negotiate. I use the word 'typically'. You should be aware that often times deals are negotiated differently based on a load of factors that you will probably never be privy to, but my point here is that 'typical' may not be 'default'. For example, agents are often asked to deduct production expenses from what we commission. So for example, if the guarantee is $100,000 and they ask us to deduct $25,000 per show towards their production, we would only commission the remaining $75,000. Or there may be a commission deal in place. Basically just remember not to assume anything as ....

There is nothing set in stone.

Let's get back to the process.

The artist wants to tour. The show needs to be worked out.

INITIAL COSTINGS

Several decisions need to be made before a tour can be costed.

What is the concept for the live show?

Where will the artist play (what markets) and in what size venues?

How big will the production be?

How long will the show be?

What types of production will be used?

The manager will consult and advise the artist on all of these questions and maybe bring in a creative team to work on the concept. Obviously this is all predicated on there being a market for the artist. For a veteran performer, this may be assumed and it may be Arenas or even stadiums, or will the artist want an intimate show and go back to theatres? For a beginner, it might be small clubs or even taking a support gig to gain exposure.

This consultation and advice for the artist is based on experience and also on offers that the agent has gotten from promoters.

THE OFFER

Promoters like everyone else in this group are wanting to find the next big thing and have them play in their markets and venues. The back and forth between agents and promoters is a series of offers and counters. An agent may represent a very popular artist and then use this fact as leverage to get a promoter to make an offer on a new artist. This topic could fill a book so we will leave it alone. You just need to be aware of the process.

Once the agent has offers in a market then it is time to take these to the manager with a view to putting together a routing that will work. The manager now has an idea of projected income so now a proper initial budget can be put together. From here the process needs to be flexible as things often change and if they change costs then they change your job, so hopefully you are included in these discussions about the routing as mentioned above, as well as the venue type.

Once the routing is agreed, and the show design is underway, the budget can be started on.

THE TOUR BUDGET

An artist will now need the services of their PM to prepare a budget for the tour. It may be that the PM was already involved in the design stage. Always a good idea as their advice and experience can really help to make sure the show is not too much of anything bad … big, heavy, or too expensive. This is dealt with in previous chapters, suffice to say here that it is an important time for you. Obviously if the show is already a known quantity then the design process is not required, and the budget can be put together quickly. Some artists will tour on the same or similar show for a while. Some artists like to change things a lot, and so you need to be ready.

Compile all your costs for the tour and present the budget to management. Different organisations do this differently. Some will expect you to use your own spreadsheet and populate it with every associated production tour expense. Others may prefer you to use their template. And still others may wish for you just to send all the bids/quotes directly to them and they will compile the actual budget.

THE DEAL

As mentioned previously, you are not involved in this side of the business, but it is important that you understand how the deal is structured. A standard show deal is usually based on a guarantee of some sort versus a percentage of net box office receipts minus verified expenses related to the show.

It might look like this: $100,000 guaranteed versus 90 percent of Net Box Office Receipts (minus the show expenses).

With a guarantee in place all the risk lies with the promoter = The artist will earn at least $100,000 if they sell only 1 ticket or a venue sell out. Once the full promoter profit is reached then every dollar either earned or spent is split 90/10 (Artist=$.90/ Promoter=$.10).

SHOW COSTS

As stated above, the show costs are the local costs incurred that are essential for the execution of the show. A very basic way of understanding what is and what is not a show cost, is highlighted by the word 'local'. You could also say that all the costs that are incurred as a result of the technical, hospitality, and security riders are what make up the list of show costs in the main. But like so much in the business, there are often exceptions; for example, sometimes artist production (touring so not local) or a part of it, may be accepted as part of the deal structure.

COVID

As I finish writing this book in June 2021, there is much discussion in our industry about how the COVID-19 pandemic will impact our business upon our return to work. We do not really know the answers fully, but there is a belief that we may well have lost a percentage of our skilled workforce to other careers or jobs. It may well be that COVID becomes a line item on our budgets for the foreseeable future. I hope that these questions are fully resolved for you by the time you are working, but be aware of this time in our history and once the economic ramifications are fully known, understand how we got there. Just another prompt from me to make sure that a broad knowledge of how the industry economics work is part of your learning to be a successful PM.

FESTIVALS

Here with the festival the economics change. It could be argued that in part the modern festival exists today as a push back against the way the economics of regular touring was structured. As agents were put under pressure to make more money, deals were tightened. In many cases agents pushed the deals to 95/5 and then the only way a promoter could make good money was to sell out every show. If you think that over the course of a year not every show was going to sell out, then the risk was seriously high. This was/is not good economics when one party leaves the transaction unsatisfied. But promoters kept stepping up to take on tours because that is the nature of the game ... it is competitive gambling in one sense. In the early 1990s, whole world tours were bought from artists and then a worldwide promoter would on sell the shows to local promoters squeezing them hard. This was not a good situation ... again not a healthy economic relationship, but the seeds were sown here for what became a new 'corporate' style of promotion.

A festival promoter builds their own show and offers flat fees to the artists. Yes these are in effect guarantees but the potential for greater profit is there for the promoter as there is no fundamental change to the financial relationship when the show sells out, or gets past 90 percent in sales. Yes, there are other side deals made with artists who can help a festival show to sell out; bonuses and such ... but the overall financial situation is kinder for the promoter. They still have all the risk but the profits are theirs.

The other big deal for the festival promoter is the financial control of the very profitable income streams not related to the artist; the bar, other concessions and the festival merchandise. There are also many sponsorship opportunities for the festival if its brand is strong. These options there for the festival promoter which do not usually present for the traditional solo show promoter.

All of what you have just read is what the industry knew as normal for the past half century plus. What we have today for many if not the majority of tours, festivals, and shows are a dominance by the corporate promoter. Their business model is different. You may well be playing in a venue that is owned by the promoter, who is making money from the car park and who is promoting the festival down the street at the same time. All this is beyond the pay grade of the PM, but it is important to understand how the game was played, how it is changing, and if, in fact, it is the same game.

NOTE

1   **This Business of Concert Promotion and Touring**
   Ray Waddell, Rich Barnett and Jake Berry Billboard Books 2007

Health and Safety

This is a huge topic. I will cover how it affects production management very briefly here and strongly encourage you to learn what is required of you in your region. Basically, it is the law that employers and their agents (you) at all times provide a workplace for employees and contractors that is safe, and does not introduce unacceptable risk to the audience.

As you go around the world you do find an enormous disparity in health and safety regulations. It would indeed be a nice thing if there could be a standard worldwide but this is likely impossible as the law seldom crosses borders easily; so currently you will need to study and understand what is required for each region as you go. Obviously on a tour the local promoters and their reps will be across this subject in relation to your engagement, but it is part of your skill set to understand your role in this provision of a safe workplace. In most countries now there are severe penalties for individuals and corporations who ignore or fail to deliver the acceptable standard of safety.

You must be very clear that this is a topic that you cannot ignore.

Let us look into how it impacts your role as a production manager (PM). I am going to highlight just three documents, here in this chapter, and for you to study further. Reading them will serve you well.

The Occupational Safety and Health Act was passed in 1970 in the United States and the Health and Safety at Work, etc. Act was passed in 1974 in the United Kingdom. In 1973 the Sports Ground Safety Authority (SGSA) published the 'Guide to Safety at Sports Grounds' known as The Green Guide. The SGSA was set up as the UK Government's advisor on safety at sports grounds. Definitely focused on the stadia industry this guide gave venue operators a broad plan of managing their crowds safely, but also concerning itself with the fine details such as aisle widths, fire and emergency evacuation plans, down to the numbers of toilets required for the capacity, etc.

In 1999, the famous Purple Guide was published by the Events Industry Forum (UK). This was specifically for the Events Industry. Someone smart had finally written it all

DOI: 10.4324/9781003231349-23

down to respond to the various acts of legislation and to the workplace changes that society was requiring. The Purple Guide was/is a comprehensive guide for the live event professional. Currently running at 33 chapters it covers everything from the legislation, transport management, and amusements, to crowd management and barriers. New chapters are added on an ongoing basis with planning for events with COVID one of the latest at the time of my writing this.

In the United States it was in 2013 that the excellent Event Safety Guide was published by the Event Safety Alliance. It is, like the Purple Guide, a guidebook for event industry professionals. The ESA guide is seriously comprehensive at over 350 pages. It does cover pretty much every issue and aspect of this topic, from Rigging safety through Un-ticketed Events to Bomb threats; both indoors and outdoors. The Event Safety Alliance is currently steering their guidance through the American National Standards Institute (ANSI) to elevate the work from a guidance to a standard.

Both of these guides are being continually updated online and could be considered living documents. You can subscribe to them and I strongly recommend that you do.

These guides and other published works, both private and government issued, are invaluable tools for you to have as you progress in your career. They will keep you up to date with the changes in the law that you must be aware of as a supervisor of workers. At the back of this book I have listed other works published in this field, which are well worth reading and having in your work library.

Let us talk about the very basics of this enormous subject for a bit and how it will impact your job. Firstly, understand that, although we as an industry can write books and guides on how to work safely, the various governments around the world have often proven that, they would prefer to lump us in with the construction industry (in the case of the UK) and not consider us to be a separate concern. This below comes directly from the UK's Health and Safety Executive's website (hse.gov.uk).

> *The Construction (Design and Management) Regulations 2015 (CDM 2015) apply to all construction projects, including those undertaken in the entertainment industry. A project includes all the planning, design and management tasks associated with construction work. For example, the building, fitting out and taking down of temporary structures for TV, film and theatre productions and live events.*
>
> *CDM 2015 makes the general duties of the Health and Safety at Work etc Act 1974 more specific. They complement the general Management of Health and Safety at Work Regulations 1999 and integrate health and safety into the management of construction projects.*

The fact that they do this 'lumping together' will make your job harder because it may not be readily apparent that rules created for an entirely different industry from yours are actually legally relevant to you in your workplace. CDM 2015 was written for the construction industry. There are obviously similarities with the work done in both our industry and in construction, but as the HSE itself acknowledges, the risks are at different levels. The industry needs to work with the authorities (which it is doing) to make sure that we do not get regulated out of a job. This important work is being done by a few dedicated organisations around the globe that need to be supported by the industry. It is important that you contribute where you are able.

I have three pieces of advice here.

1. If you start out with a view to having a safe show and not a show about safety, you will do ok.

2. Stay out in front and keep abreast of what is happening in the world of health and safety regulation.

3. Most importantly, understand the possible human cost of an accident.

There are the essential, logical, and usually obvious safety issues that we all understand. Try examining a load in from a hazard identification perspective. It is not hard to identify what is risky and what is not and seek to put in place certain measures to minimise these risks. Securing ramps to docks, having spotters work when vehicles are moving. Issuing workers with personal protective equipment (PPE). All very basic and fundamental measures that we are used to and understand.

Although you would hope that this is not so, there are places (countries/regions) where workplace safety is not a huge priority. This should not change the way you work when you are in these places. You should still 'secure that ramp to that dock' and implement all the other sensible risk management measures regardless.

Then there are the places where the safety 'extremists' live. People can make Occupational Health and Safety (OH&S) difficult indeed. It is a fundamental premise of OH&S that it is there to make what we do, safe, rather than set out to change what we do. For example, a fire eater in a circus is performing what is essentially an unsafe practice. The extremist would have you stop the fire eater performing altogether. The sensible OH&S operative rather would seek to make the performance AS SAFE AS IS POSSIBLE, by first identifying the risks and then seeking either to remove them completely or, if this is not possible, to reduce the risk as much as is possible…then to maintain a system of review to ensure that the risks stay mitigated. You can see here where the extremist and the sensible OH&S operatives diverge. You would be well advised to dwell somewhere in between the two extremes. Learn about risk identification and management and supervise your production in a consistently safe manner and you will be OK. *If you are unsure, always consult with a safety professional.*

If you consider that the primary driver of most health and safety law is risk to individuals and its mitigation, with the failure of this leading to the apportioning of liability, then you can start to understand the motives and constructs presented to you by OH&S professionals. Who is responsible? What is required of that responsible person so that they can be covered by insurance. From these questions come the rules and laws that we are governed by. Consider, however, the catalyst here. Most of these guides and organisations within our industry spring up as a response to an accident, a tragedy. The Event Safety Alliance formed in the wake of the Indiana State Fair tragedy in 2011 where seven people lost their lives because of a stage roof collapse. The Purple Guide was written in the aftermath of the tragic deaths of two patrons at the Monsters of Rock Festival at Donington in 1988.

The OH&S law is the law and we all have to abide by it even when/if we do not agree with it. You can still follow the law in workplace health and safety without completely surrendering to the extremists. Ask questions and remain informed and up to date. Engage with the OH&S professionals that you encounter and do not treat them as adversaries. Find out what they are seeking to achieve and see where you can assist. Be involved.

I am not going to dive into risk matrices or contractor control methods or the many other topics in OH&S. It is all there for you in the aforementioned guides, on government websites and in the various other articles and books written on the topic. There is so much information to digest so I suggest that you start now and keep it as a part of your ongoing education.

Before I end this brief chapter, I am going to urge you to have a good long think about why we have the OH&S rules and remember that in the history of our industry the tragedies that triggered these changes had a human cost to them. It is often hard to get someone to really understand something they have no actual experience of, but you just have to look at that video of the Indiana State Fair roof coming down to feel it a little. As a friend, who is expert in this field, said to me. Those patrons went to that gig with the expectation of a fun day, immersed in their culture. Instead they were terrified and seven of them died with many others injured.

Be engaged and pay attention. You have a responsibility under the law but also just as a caring human.

MENTAL HEALTH

Finally, industry (and society in general) is bringing this topic to the fore. Why is this topic in the OH&S chapter? The understanding and the maintenance of the mental health of the people you supervise in your workplace is as fundamental to overall health and safety as the very obvious measures like PPE or the assessment of risk from working at heights. As the stigma attached to suffering from mental health issues diminishes, we can put in place the appropriate measures to help manage this for our workers and in doing so make the workplace healthier. As a PM, you must be aware that adverse mental health is a risk to for the workplace and just like any other risk, you must work to reduce or remove it. With the unemotional OH&S language aside now, as we all know, many people really struggle to get through their day because of mental health or the lack of it. Think for one minute about how we work in a pressured environment and we are driven every day to meet a deadline that cannot be delayed. It is a tough enough workplace to succeed in for the healthiest of us.

Someone who is suffering needs expert advice and care. You are most likely not a clinician. There are Mental Health First Aid courses that you can do, and these are great to help you identify if someone you work with is suffering. Here now is the important bit. Just as what we know as regular first aid is designed to be implemented until the patient can get actual medical help, so to with Mental Health First Aid. As I said, get a person suffering some expert help ASAP. You will have done your part in identifying the problem.

As with all the topics within Health and Safety, this is not something you can ignore or leave. You must be aware and engaged. It is part of you duty of care as a supervisor in a workplace.

Sustainability, Diversity, and Inclusion

I write this chapter, in the second year of the COVID-19 pandemic, just as the United States market is beginning to open up again finally. There has been a lot of discussion during this down time about the issues that we need to deal with as we return to work and in the future. Broadly, they seemed to have fallen into three main categories.

- Sustainability
- Diversity Equity and Inclusion
- Mental Health

I will deal with the first two in this chapter. Mental Health is covered briefly in the Health and Safety chapter preceding.

I am by no means an expert in any of these areas. I have been involved in these industry discussions however and so will offer a brief overview as to how I see we, as an industry, and you and I, as production managers, can respond to these vital issues.

Firstly let's look at working more sustainably. You will hear a lot that our industry is relatively quite a small emitter. Whilst that may be true, it is also not the point. For two reasons.

Firstly, we are a *relatively* small emitter that is true. However, we are also a wasteful industry, and that is the point we should be looking at. One fact I have learned in my research made me sit up and take notice. Over the event season of 2017/2018 in the United Kingdom a study was done into diesel generator use at outdoor events. There were some 7000 licensed events for that period from the massive festivals to the local council fete. This study found that the amount of diesel fuel that was WASTED over this

DOI: 10.4324/9781003231349-24

period had a value of NINETY MILLION POUNDS. The scientists who conduct this research told me that their jaws dropped as well. I have a link to this research in Further Reading. I don't think I really need to add anything to this statistic. We need to get our house in order.

The second reason concerns the reach our industry has. If you think that the ten most popular artists in the world have a social media audience in the billions, you should straight away see how we can affect change. The big issue behind this is that for live music the biggest emitter is actually the audience. But the concert and festival going public are the ones who can demand change from their governments; better public transport to the venues, more sustainable practices generally, and our influential clients can urge them to do as much. If the patrons at our festivals and concerts are seeing good examples from us, seeing that the music industry is working sustainably then it should encourage them to join in, both in their own practices but also in how they vote and make their voice heard for those in power.

At the beginning of my last tour, I asked the catering coordinator to look at ways that we could reduce the amount of waste that the tour produced. The first thing we did was to cut out the use of single use water bottles. We gave every crew member a nice reusable water bottle and had five gallon jugs of water positioned around the gig and on every bus. We were not pioneers in this with many tours having made this one waste reduction effort already, but we made a choice to change. Our crew all got behind it and we not only avoided using and then discarding thousands of single use water bottles, the crew were also better hydrated on average. It was indeed gratifying to see such positives from just this one small change.

There are other very obvious areas where touring organisations can affect change and adopt more sustainable practices. If you just spend a few minutes thinking about all the different ways we use electricity and how many of those sources are dirty. Diesel generators are one of the dirtiest emitters and the music industry has traditionally used a LOT of diesel generators. The most obvious are the ones used at festival sites, but just think that every tour bus and tour truck in the biggest market (the USA) also has one. That is a lot of dirty power.

Much good work is being done to reduce the emissions at festival sites in particular with some really smart people 'crunching the numbers' in power consumption, waste reduction, plastic usage, and other areas to make a measurable difference.

There is also a move to make sure that shore power (grid power circuit provide by a venue for a tour vehicle) is available in the future for EVERY tour bus and truck. Most often in the past you could usually put all the buses on shore power but the trucks would have to run their generators, so this would be such a good thing to be able to reduce or completely remove.

As a veteran industry professional, I have a feeling that here I might just be preaching to the choir. Young people across the world in every walk of life are demanding change to save this planet. So in conclusion, I will say be encouraged that this music industry is starting to change and with enthusiastic professionals like yourself coming up and getting involved, we are at least going to keep moving in this right direction, reducing the industry's footprint and influencing the audience to do the same to theirs.

DIVERSITY AND INCLUSION

The music industry suffers from a lack of diversity and it is, like many industries, guilty of not being inclusive enough. Historically, dominated by white males, the industry will benefit enormously from a more diverse workforce. I believe that finally there is broad support for this change, but we must make sure that it does not just become something that happened during the pandemic and then faded away. The momentum that has started must be kept going. I do think that it is also very important to understand that there has been work carried on in this area long before the most recent wave of social justice and gender equality movements. Let us not forget that many passionate people have been working for years to develop educational and training resources for our industry. I can imagine the wry smiles on the faces of these pioneers as they finally see this broad wave of assistance heading their way. I for one do not wish to see the baby thrown out with the bath water and would hope that these new movements engage with rather than seek to replace the work that has been done.

In the short term the way people are being hired for roles in this business is what needs to change. Currently, people find out about jobs by either word or mouth or via job post sites that are accessible to those that are either already in the business or they know someone who is. These 'methods' are flawed for very obvious reasons. If we can change the mindset of the hirer and at the same time, provide he or she with the tools to cast a wider employment net then we are doing something new.

For the long term it will be through establishing many more accredited educational offerings for young people. We should concentrate on developing a strong feeder for the industry that teaches young people of any colour or gender the skills that the industry needs its young professionals to have. These are not easy jobs, but they must be accessible to anyone who wishes to learn them.

We have not had any sort of formal *industry wide* method for young people to access jobs in the business. Smaller private colleges and academies as well as some vendor training programmes have been carrying the torch to date. I applaud the efforts of these and believe that now, we can have them leave the silos and work with the broader industry to finally overcome this big and important issue.

It is heartening to see that the industry leaders are now engaging with universities and colleges, both private and community and as long as this continues with a solid commitment on both sides we will see things change.

Bibliography

CONCERT TOUR AND PRODUCTION MANAGEMENT

John Vasey   Focal Press   1998

THIS BUSINESS OF CONCERT PROMOTION AND TOURING

Ray Waddell, Rich Barnett, and Jake Berry   Billboard Books   2007

HEALTH AND SAFETY ASPECTS IN THE LIVE MUSIC INDUSTRY

Chris Kemp and Iain Hill   Entertainment and Technology Press   2004

ENERGY IMPACTS FROM FESTIVAL AND TOURING PRODUCTIONS

Hope Solutions and ZAP Concepts   2020

Glossary

Agent: The individual or company that is retained by an artist to book shows or tours.

Backstage: The secure area from the down stage edge to the rear of the venue including the dressing rooms and the docks. Everywhere that is not front of house.

Backline: The band equipment. The crew that work directly with the musicians. The set of amplifiers and risers and instruments set in place on stage.

Band Gear: The equipment used directly by the artist/band in the show as well as the supporting tech equipment, including instruments, amplifiers, workstations, etc.

Barrier: Refers to the crowd control fence that runs across the front of a stage as well as being used in various configurations throughout a venue or festival site to control crowd movement.

Boneyard: Refers to the area allocated by the site to house the stillages and storage for the steel system as well as other department storage.

CAD: 'Computer aided design' commonly refers to the different drawing programs and to the drawings themselves. Often ticketing companies and venues refer to the sale diagrams as a CAD.

Call: The time that a shift of work starts, or the time that the entourage moves (e.g. Show Call, Bus Call).

Camp: A term that refers to the organisation that works for an artist. Will include all the touring personnel, as well as the management team at the artist's base.

Carp: A carpenter who on a touring crew looks after the installation and removal of the set.

Catering: The dining room where the touring party and ancillary staff are fed. Sometimes this is toured as part of the production.

Changeover: The swap of gear from one act to another on the same stage (e.g. from the support to the main act).

Crew: The group of individuals employed by one artist that travel and work together under the direction of the production manager.

Deck: The stage.

DSE: Acronym for down stage edge.

FOH: An acronym for 'Front of House'. Refers to both all of the venue that is NOT backstage and also to the mixing and control position in front of the stage.

Fork: A forklift truck.

GIG: Refers to both a show and also a job (as in 'I got a gig' which means I gained employment).

Grid: The network of beams in a venue or stage roof from where the rig is flown.

Labour: Refers to the group of individuals employed locally as a workforce controlled by the Production to install and remove the show.

Line check: The process where the audio crew go through every input to make sure everything is working. The final line check takes place during the changeover just before the show.

Local Crew: The team of local stagehands, riggers, and other staff that come in to work with the tour in each venue.

Mark out: Sometimes called the 'chalk', it is the process of drawing out the rigging points on the floor of the venue in their exact position for the riggers to connect to the venue grid via the chain hoist and point rigging.

Merch: A shortening of Merchandise.

Monitor Engineer: The operator of the monitor system.

Monitor system: The audio system that is installed on the stage for the performers to listen to, as opposed to the audience. Sometimes just called 'monitors'.

PA: Acronym for 'Public Address', refers to the main audio system.

Pack: The way and order the various road cases go together in a truck or container for transporting.

PM: Acronym for 'Production Manager'.

Point: One of the many connections between the flown rigs and the grid of the venue.

Pre-rig: A separate rigging call scheduled prior to the regular load in to save or gain time.

Production Rehearsal: A rehearsal for the entire show.

Promoter: The individual or company that puts on the concert or festival show or tour.

Punter: A ticket buying patron or audience member.

Rider: A document or addendum to a performance contract that outlines the various requirements of an artist. Common types of riders are legal, technical, hotel, security, and hospitality.

Rig: This term refers to collection of equipment that combined perform a function for a show (e.g. a guitar rig, the lighting rig, etc.).

Rigger: An individual trained to install the rigging of a live show in the roof of a venue or festival.

Routing: A list of the shows to be played on a tour listed in chronological order with cities and venues.

Run: A leg of a tour. A series of shows.

Runner: A local (usually) staff member employed to run errands for the production.

Set: The usually bespoke structure that an artist performs on and around.

SFX: Acronym for 'special effects' refers to pyrotechnics, CO_2 gases, or other effects that are part of a show.

Sightline: A line drawn on a seating plan to indicate the different view perspectives of the different seats with regard to placement of the stage and the production equipment.

Siteco: A shortening of the term Site Coordinator (Chapter 6).

SL: A shortening of Stage Left.

SM: An acronym for 'Stage Manager'.

Spec: Shortening for 'specification' used in conjunction with the relevant department name to refer to the list of equipment that is either provided or required by the production (e.g. Audio spec).

SR: A shortening of Stage Right.

Stage plot: The map drawn (usually to scale) to indicate the positions of the equipment on the stage.

Support: A term that refers to the opening act on a show.

Tech: The Rock jargon for a technician.

Teching: The actions performed by a tech.

TM: An acronym for 'Tour Manager'.

Trailer: A Pantech of varying lengths, containing all the tour production equipment, towed by the tour trucks.

Vendor: A company providing production goods and services to the music industry.

Index

Milton Keynes UK
Ingram Content Group UK Ltd.
UKHW020846141024
449569UK00003B/89

9 781032 138923